The Ebenezer Stone:

Alaska Journey Home

Jean Mallory

First Edition

Cover: The cover was designed by Tara Martinez, Digital Design Class, Haney Technical School, Lynn Haven, Florida. Front cover photography by Suzanne Vann.

The events in this book are based on true experiences and situations. A few names and events have been changed or altered for my own reasons.

All Scripture quotations are taken from:
The Holy Bible
King James Version

ISBN: 978-1-84961-183-1
Real Time Publishing
Limerick Ireland

Dedication

...Unto Him that loved us, and washed us from our sins in His own blood. Revelation 1:5b

Acknowledgments

Thank you to those who helped, prayed and encouraged me through the process of 'remembering' and putting these thoughts in book form. Beverly, I was so grateful for your picture album and Kelly for your postcards.

Thank you to The Digital Design class at Haney Technical Center, instructor Jason Heath and Suzanne Vann for the beautiful picture on the front cover.

A very special thank you for editorial help and suggestions:
Pastor T.A. Green
Ann Dyess
Dave Hanson
Tamara Heptinstall
Bernice (Granny) Riley
Janet Nicolet

Contents

Introduction

In the course of my work, I entered a small business one day and sat down waiting to be called to the back office. Directly in front of the receptionist's desk on the floor was a very large rock. I thought it was a bit strange and very unexpected, but then I noticed the sign above the rock on the front of the desk.

The Ebenezer Stone

Then Samuel took a stone, and set it between Mizpeh and Shen, and called the name of it Ebenezer, saying, Hitherto hath the LORD helped us. I Samuel 7:12

What a wonderful scripture! I pondered this and thought how very much it applied to my life. I couldn't wait to get home and study that scripture in depth. That incident was over a year ago and I still can't stop thinking about how that verse applies to me.

A few months ago I realized that this scripture would be the basis of a book; a book that I have put off writing for a long time. A book about how the Lord has personally helped me through situations in my life, and specifically during the time my husband was called home to Heaven while we were a long way from our earthly home. It was his 'Alaska Journey Home'.

The original journal of that trip has been lost. A tremendous amount of time has been spent researching the beautiful state of Alaska in order to retrace our travels.

Thankfully, I still have all the pictures and they were imprinted with the dates. Some family members and friends also shared the postcards they received from us. Please ignore my sloppy handwriting on the postcards and letters. My handwriting has never been the best and I usually wrote during the hours when he drove, so we were often moving on bumpy roads. I was also very distracted when there was so much to look at.

I really was rather amazed at all the memories that came back about specific places and events. Ebay yielded a 1988 Milepost magazine along with old maps and other research items. A 1989 calendar was helpful. The Milepost was one year off but helped a lot.

It was often very poignant dredging the memories out of my mind, but in doing so I proved just how important it is to 'remember what God has done.' It has deepened and enriched my spiritual life to remember again just how great God is and how much He cares about every detail in the lives of His children.

Chapter One
I Samuel 7

REMEMBER

Some trust in chariots, and some in horses: but we will remember the name of the LORD our God.
Psalms 20:7

It's easy to trust in our strength, our resources, our bank account or our capabilities. If we remember to trust in our God first, He will use what we have to bring about His will. Just always remember to rely on Him and go to Him first.

Before I can begin the story of our journey, I need to share a little background on the chapter of I Samuel 7. Since this is the story that my inspiration came from, it's important to know just what had happened before Samuel uttered that profound statement.

In the book of I Samuel Chapter 7, a specific story is told. The Israelites had been oppressed by the Philistines for forty years and the ark had been at Kirjath-Jearim for twenty years. God allowed this oppression because of Israel's idolatry.

This chapter is a great Old Testament revival chapter. Previously the people believed their hope was in recovering the ark. They thought that having the ark with them would lead them to freedom from oppression. In verse 2, it tells that all the people *"lamented after the Lord."* That's when they no longer placed their hope in the ark, but turned to the one who could really help them.

Samuel recognized the sincerity of their cry. He gave them God's conditional answer. Remember all the promises in God's Word are conditional. They always have an "if." First we do our part, and then God will do His.

And Samuel spake unto all the house of Israel, saying, If ye do return unto the LORD with all your hearts, then put away the strange gods and Ashtaroth from among you, and prepare your hearts unto the LORD, and serve him only: and he will deliver you out of the hand of the Philistines. 1 Samuel 7:3

First of all, they had to return to the Lord with <u>all</u> their hearts, nothing held back. Then they needed to put away the strange idols completely. We still have strange idols today, usually innocent-seeming things or habits that draw us away from God.

The next thing was to prepare their hearts. Only a set and steadfast heart toward God will stand and be strong and not be swayed by the things of the world. We prepare our hearts by prayer, reading God's Word and constantly re-committing our lives to Him and His way.

These things are necessary for us today to live holy lives. We must have true conviction and repentance and then seek God daily for His will in our lives.

When these changes were made, Samuel gathered them together to pray for them. They fasted that day and Samuel poured out water in a ceremony, perhaps to show the pouring out of their hearts in repentance before Him.

When the Philistines heard of the gathering, they perceived it as a threat and prepared to attack. The Israelites were afraid, and implored Samuel to continue praying for them. Samuel sacrificed a lamb for a burnt offering and when the Philistines drew near, his prayers were answered. God spoke with a loud, mighty voice of thunder. The enemy was confused and the Lord won the battle for the Israelites.

Then Samuel took a stone, and set it between Mizpeh and Shen, and called the name of it Ebenezer, saying, Hitherto hath the Lord helped us. I Samuel 7:12

Samuel recognized what a great thing the Lord had done. He set a stone between Mizpeh and Shen for a **remembrance** forever. The victory had come through the divine aid of God. They all knew it and they knew how important it was to remember the victory.

Remembering what a mighty, mighty God we serve by recalling what He has done in the past is the basis of our faith for the future. The future in this life is very uncertain, but knowing God is here and will be with us in every situation gives us hope and peace in our souls.

'**Hitherto**' **or** '**until this time**,' or up until now simply means to **look back and remember** what happened from then until now. It is so very important to '**remember**', to **remember** what He has done for others, and **remember** what He has done for you.

Remember how the waters of Jordan parted when the priests stepped in. **Remember** how the bonds of the prisoners were broken and the door opened when they were in jail. **Remember** how the dead were raised. **Remember** all these 'impossible' things. **Remember** how 'impossible' it was when He saved you?

In that darkest hour when we feel that God is far away...remember. Paul was greatly concerned about the Thessalonian Christians when they were being severely persecuted. How relieved he was when Timothy reported to him that they were doing well and had good remembrance of all he had taught them, *I Thessalonians 3:6.* He had warned them that they would be persecuted, and they also watched as Paul himself faced persecution. **Remembering** gave them the determination to stand when the same thing came to them.

Hitherto, 'up until now', the Lord has been my solid rock and has helped me in every way, through every situation. I believe He will continue to help until my journey on this earth is complete. Perhaps in reading this you will realize that He has helped you also, and you can gain strength from **remembering** just what He has done.

Every chapter of this book will begin with a scripture about **remembering.** It's often necessary to look back and **remember** just what God did for us last week, last month, last year and many years prior to that.

"If you don't rely upon what God has done for you in the past, there is no future, for the whole of Christianity is to grow in Christ." Pastor Donald W. Shoots

Chapter Two
Depending on Him

REMEMBER

And the bow shall be in the cloud; and I will look upon it, that I may remember the everlasting covenant between God and every living creature of all flesh that is upon the earth. Genesis 9:16

Certain things help us to remember. Looking upon a precious child's or grandchild's face, one who is a miracle because he was never supposed to survive, but God intervened. Keep a journal or write notes of important happenings. We think we can remember, but it gets more difficult as time goes by. Take lots of pictures and save them.

My husband and I had a wonderful marriage. There were a few ups and very few downs. For the most part, our marriage progressed on a steady, even keel that was comfortable to both of us. After very difficult first marriages, it was fantastic to find soul mates who shared the same biblical views of marriage.

His full name was Adolph Mallory. He was a small child during WWII and it was no surprise he rarely used his first name with the German dictator in power. Everyone called him by his last name and I did the same. Currently Mallory is a very popular first name for girls, but it wasn't at that time.

Mallory was a strong Christian and relied daily on God to lead him. He pastored a church for many years until his divorce. He had preached against divorce for years, and when he found himself in that situation, he no longer felt worthy to lead others and resigned from the church.

I had accepted Christ as my Savior but like many other people, I had a very shallow surface knowledge of the Lord. I did believe but I don't think I had ever truly believed with my whole heart and learned to trust God with everything. *Mark 1:15* tells us to repent <u>and</u> believe. If you separate the two, you won't have faith and you must have faith to live the Christian life and have a relationship with

Christ. Instead of a relationship with Him and relying on Him, I relied mostly on myself.

In my first marriage I was a military wife for 17 years. With my husband constantly volunteering for overseas assignments, I filled the role of mom and dad to our three daughters. Every year I became more independent.

Believing in fidelity, it is a painful situation, when one partner choses to take their vows lightly. We drifted far apart until there was really nothing left of our marriage. On his few trips home, I tried to salvage our home. He grew more unhappy and hard to live with. When he began to show that frustration by being unfair to the children, I knew it was over. He was extremely relieved when I asked him if he wanted out of the marriage and admitted he had another family in that far-away country. The marriage ended.

The girls and I moved to another state and found a place to live. I found work managing a small convenience store. After a few weeks I recognized the regular customers and realized a certain gentleman came in several times a day. He liked to hang around and talk.

The one thing I was definitely not interested in was a relationship with anyone. I was a pretty independent military wife because my husband chose to be gone most of the time. Now I certainly wasn't interested in anyone else, and all I wanted to do was take care of my girls and carve out some kind of future career for myself.

He was an interesting man, and had a sad story of his own. I enjoyed talking to him when the store wasn't busy. He had asked me to go out, but with the responsibility of two teenagers and a two-year old, I really wasn't interested in anything more than friendship, I thought.

There came a day when he didn't come in the store like he usually did. I just figured he was busy, not wanting to admit to myself that I missed him. On the third day of his not appearing, one of his daughters came in the store and mentioned that he had been in the hospital. The sudden certainty hit me that I cared about this man. He was a welcome sight the next day when he once again came into the store. I accepted his invitation to take our girls out to breakfast on my next day off.

He was twelve years older than me, a very solid and dependable man. Most of all, I admired the steadfast Christianity that was obvious in his life. That was something I had never been around.

One night when I was taking out boxes to the dumpster just before closing, a man came out of the darkness and tackled me. I squirmed away and jumped up screaming and hitting. He ran off, but I got a glimpse of his face and realized it was an emotionally-disturbed young man who came in the store often. It was a terrifying experience and my first thought was to call Mallory.

I wasn't hurt except for some scrapes, but I just really needed someone to lean on. He came to the store when the police arrived and by the time I finished with the police report, I was still shaking. I remember how comforting it was just to have his calm, stable reassurance close by. At his advice I applied for a different type of job, but we still saw each other very often.

That's how it began, and months later we decided on a small wedding during the time his son would be home on leave, with just the family in attendance.

We began attending church with his family. Some churches in our area were not kind to a divorced former pastor dating a divorced woman, even if the divorces were for Biblical reasons. We were married in the small church we had attended for months. After the ceremony, the pastor smilingly told us to go and find a good church to be part of and where we could work. Realizing that we weren't wanted there, we found one that would accept us.

We began our blended marriage with five teenagers, a twelve-year-old and a three-year-old in the house. He also had three married children. It was quite a houseful. Every year someone would get married or move out on their own. One daughter went to Heaven at the age of twenty, with the same genetic heart problems that ran through the family.

In the third year of our marriage, Mallory suffered a very severe heart attack. We knew he had an inherited heart condition because of previous problems. This time he remained in the hospital for several weeks. He suffered from severe cardiomyopathy. His heart was greatly enlarged and very often the beat was irregular. At one point in the out-of-town hospital after this attack, the doctors asked me to call the family because it was doubtful he would make it much longer.

It was at this time, that I comprehended just how lacking I was in faith and knowledge and how shallow my spiritual life was. The girls had rented a motel room so we could take turns resting. Since I had not left the hospital for days, the family insisted I go and get a little rest while they stayed with him. I knew I wouldn't stay there long but I agreed to go.

The shower was wonderful after trying to keep clean in the waiting room bathroom. Instead of sleeping, I knelt and began reading the Gideon Bible placed in the room. I tearfully surrendered everything I had to God's perfect will. Promising to always be obedient and do whatever He asked of me, I begged Him for my husband's life to be extended. But I promised to accept His will, whatever it was. A complete change came over me, and I knew I had reached a much deeper level in my relationship with the Lord.

Many prayed for him during this time. Mallory prayed also when he was awake. He felt his earthly affairs were not in order and he still had things that needed to be completed.

The doctors were quite surprised when he regained his strength and was able to be discharged from the hospital. They told him to quit working and just try and not do much of anything. He did retire from work, but enjoyed doing many things like raising bees, gardening, fishing, hunting and exploring the river and swamps which were part of our backyard. When we went back for follow-up appointments, the doctor shook his head and said, "I don't know what you're doing but keep on doing it!"

That severe heart attack and his miraculous recovery were vivid examples of one time that God helped us. My part required totally committing my life to the direction of God and completely trusting His will and not ours.

Mallory was not completely healed. He had to retire from his work. He still lived with that heart condition daily. We moved to one of his favorite places, a place on the river, where he could do most of the things he loved at his own pace. He couldn't do a lot physically. We learned to trust God for each and every day He gave us. Whenever problems came along, we knew God was our strength. He was in control and would help us through any situation.

Chapter Three
Preparing for the Journey

REMEMBER

For I will be merciful to their unrighteousness, and their sins and their iniquities will I remember no more.
Hebrews 8:12

What a wonderful thought! When we turn to Jesus and accept Him, He will forgive us so completely that He will never remember what a miserable sinner we were, or any of our sins. It helps that our past sins aren't removed from our minds. By remembering what we were, we can rejoice in what He has brought us from.

How we rejoiced and praised God for what He had done in our lives. We had difficult times like anyone else, but He was always there with us and each rough place seemed to strengthen and mature us a little more.

We celebrated fourteen years of marriage and all of its ups and downs. God blessed us with a happy home, a good church and a wonderful church family. Mallory worked in our church teaching, and he also preached in our church and others as a fill-in when needed.

I continued to work throughout those years. Our youngest daughter was in her senior year of high school and almost ready to graduate.

Mallory learned not to overdo, to rest a lot and concentrate on the things he enjoyed the most. Still, we knew the disease was progressing. He traveled very little during his lifetime and always had a dream to visit the state of Alaska as well as the western United States.

Often we discussed this and planned to go there one day, but finances and my full-time job, along with other obligations, always ended our discussions. It was just one of the things to do in the future. In the fall of 1988, we were again talking about 'the trip'.

He said "You know honey, if we don't go soon, I won't be able to go." I realized with a shock it was time to quit talking about it and make a concrete plan. That's exactly what we did!

We started planning and working on the details. Mallory loved and honored God. He preached, taught, witnessed and lived a Godly life. It seemed like God wished to give him the desire of his heart before it was time to take him home.

Thou hast given him his heart's desire, and hast not withholden the request of his lips. Psalms 21:2

An understanding boss agreed to a leave of absence for the following year. I was actually prepared to quit my job if he had not agreed. That sounds a little drastic, but we knew this trip was in God's will, and He would work out all the details.

The 401k savings yielded enough to put a down payment on a small Winnebago RV and provide for traveling money even after the penalties for early withdrawal. We purchased the RV and spent the winter months preparing for an extended trip. We took several small trips in the RV to become familiar with it. I knew I would be doing most of the driving and was grateful that it was very easy to drive.

The basic plan, subject to change of course, was to drive as we wished through the western states and take the Alcan or Alaskan Canadian highway all the way to Alaska. We would drive all over the state and include a trip to visit missionary friends in Kotzebue, which included a moose hunt. Kotzebue was only accessible by private bush plane. We planned to return home in late September or early

October by the inland ferry route to Seattle and then driving a different route home.

    We bought maps and books and made many phone calls as we planned our route. It all went so smoothly that only God could have organized it all.

    We consulted God about all aspects of this trip. Knowing He is our source and guide gave us a tremendous amount of peace over all the details. If either one of us had not felt God's peace in our hearts that day, there wouldn't have been any hesitation about cancelling the trip. It simply had to be in God's will to take on a road trip of around 6000 miles one way, and putting everything else in our lives on hold for an indefinite amount of time.

    Leaving Mallory's doctors and the security of having family and friends close by might have given us a little twinge of concern, but because of the orderly way God arranged and put the trip-planning together we truly felt peace that our steps were ordered by Him.

Because of the cost and availability of some supplies in the far northwest, we shopped for bargains on the non-perishable items. We also bought special raingear, boots and waders, knowing it rained a lot and we would be outside often.

The end of May, 1989, found us just about ready to get on the road. All the details and planning were complete for our extended journey. Our youngest daughter would stay with her sister, while she worked and saved for college in the fall. At least that's what we thought she would do, but that's another story. My mother lived right next door and would keep an eye on the place. A church friend would pay bills from our account and take care of other bookkeeping. The Sunday school class was prepared with substitute teachers.

There were no computers, cell phones or GPS devices. Maps, atlases and the 'Milepost' travel guide provided our tentative route. Now in the 21st century we are so dependent on our electronics, we wouldn't even attempt an extended trip without them. The 1989 'Milepost' proved to be a wonderful tool, giving mile-by mile-logs of all the things to look for in the Northwest.

Our Sunday school class gave us a combination 'bon voyage' and birthday party for Mallory's 60th birthday. It was an enjoyable time with friends and family. Finally, the appointed day arrived, June 9th. After prayer time, we received the peace and confirmation that God was in control and we were in His will, we pulled out of the driveway in the loaded RV and headed west.

Chapter Four
The Journey Begins, Unexpected Hazards

REMEMBER

This second epistle, beloved, I now write unto you; in both which I stir up your pure minds by way of remembrance: That ye may be mindful of the words which were spoken before by the holy prophets, and of the commandment of us the apostles of the Lord and Saviour: 2 Peter 3:1,2
In the scripture above, Peter wasn't revealing anything new, but he was reminding us to remember what had already been told. By looking back at God's Word, we can be assured that it is always dependable and accurate and it gives us a reason to live holy lives while looking towards the future.

We didn't get very far the first day. But then we really didn't have a certain number of miles to go each day. It was great to be led by God and just enjoy all the wonders He wanted to share with us.

We spent the first night at a state park in Mississippi. It was a beautiful place for novice campers to enjoy. From there we went on to Louisiana and visited his son and his family for a day or so before continuing on.

That first Sunday we visited a former pastor at his church in northern Texas. We had an enjoyable visit. We spent the night parked in the church parking lot. There were more family visits in Texas, and later Nevada, before we ventured on to the great Northwest.

Every day brought new wonders to see, and every day we felt more like seasoned travelers and relaxed in the routine of the trip. Perhaps we were too relaxed.

I was born in the west and had seen much of what there was to see, but it was always fascinating to see it anew through his eyes.

He started most of the days driving because early mornings he always felt the best. Usually he would have me take over after a couple of hours. Not driving made it easier for him to sight-see, also. We stopped whenever we chose to and looked around.

It was really hot and dry that June. We left my sister's home in Lampasas, Texas and continued our meandering trip towards the west. We had stopped somewhere in southern New Mexico for the night and the next morning Mallory started driving in the hilly country. The hills were pretty high and quite rocky.

About half way down one hill the brakes on the RV completely gave out. He did everything he knew to slow it down, but it was quite a hair-raising ride before we reached the bottom and he managed to get the vehicle stopped. A lot of frantic prayers went up during that down-hill run. What a blessing that there were no slower vehicles in front of us. It was a two-lane road without much room to maneuver.

Praising God for His protecting hand over us, we knew we would spend a little more time every day devoting everything we would face into His hands.

I think of the scripture I'm using as the inspiration for this book. The last sentence states *"Hitherto hath the Lord helped us." 1 Samuel 7:12.* Hitherto actually means 'up until this time.' The verse is reminding us to remember how He has helped us and how He will continue to help us if we remain close to Him. He certainly helped us that day and every day since.

I wonder sometimes, how many dangers he delivers us from that we don't even know about. One day just a few years ago, I was driving on a busy street and looking for my turn into a certain address. When I turned into the business and parked, another car parked right beside mine, and a young man rushed up to me as I opened the door.

"Oh, I am so sorry! I certainly didn't mean to scare you with that close call. The cuff of my pants caught on the pedal and I really thought I would hit you but somehow it didn't happen. Please forgive me. It was totally an accident because I'm a very safe driver."

I stared blankly at the young man having no idea what he was talking about. I assured him that there was no problem and I certainly didn't blame him for anything. I would never know just what a close call it was. As he went back to his car, I could only say, "Thank you, Lord, You did it again. Even though I didn't even see or feel the danger."

It was one more thing that He protected me from that I never knew about.

Back to our trip; at the bottom of the runaway hill, when we looked around, we realized the hill was the entrance to the next small town on the way. We were able to creep to a nearby mechanics shop to get the brakes repaired.

The next day after repairs were made to the brakes, we were between Tucson and Phoenix with the outside temperature at 109 degrees when the air conditioning system stopped working. The heat began to affect Mallory when we were driving through the city traffic, trying to find the Winnebago dealer. He was OK after resting in the air conditioning of the dealership while the repairs were made.

We had some generator problems along the way and managed to keep the RV dealers busy.

There was one other really frightening event that could have been disastrous if God's hand hadn't been on us. It was after we got on the Alcan (Alaskan Canadian highway) near Ft. Nelson, British Columbia. It was the last week of June and absolutely beautiful country. The road at that time was gravel all the way and very, very bumpy. The RV was really getting a workout.

We used every space to pack things, sometimes heavy things, not giving any thought that our packing could backfire on us.

Mallory happened to be driving that morning when the overhead bed above our heads suddenly fell. It didn't knock either one of us out but it hurt! Thank God for hard heads!

I managed to stand and lift the bed as he hit the brakes and pulled to the side of the road and stopped. We were unhurt but we both had lumps on our heads and stiff necks the next day. God completely protected us. Again, it was off to the next dealership for more repairs. We were very careful about what we packed on that overhead bed for the rest of the trip.

We had chips in our windshield like most of the other travelers. Some also dealt with windshield cracks from that very long rough road with hundreds of miles of gravel.

Chapter Five
Western States

REMEMBER

Yea, in the way of thy judgments, O LORD, have we waited for thee; the desire of our soul is to thy name, and to the remembrance of thee   Isaiah 26:8

Sometimes, when we are on a trip or vacation and out of our normal routine, our usual way of praying, studying and seeking God is interrupted and pushed out of the way while we pursue different activities. A determined effort must be made to continue to put God first and seek Him often, constantly asking for His leading and guiding.

I think Mallory enjoyed the western states as much as he did Alaska. He had never travelled extensively through the west and there was so much to see.

We often used less-traveled roads to seek out interesting places. In southern New Mexico, we visited White Sands National Monument, near Alamogordo.

In southern Arizona we saw so many beautiful and varied cacti. The giant saguaro cacti were his favorite. He spent a lot of time in his recliner resting at home. He loved old western movies on the television, and always spoke of the cowboy crawling across the desert, and just in time before he died, he would find a cactus that would give him the water he needed to live.

We took a lot of pictures of the desert and the cactus plants. Many scenery pictures didn't translate well into this document and had to be left out.

The saguaros often appeared as lonely, silent sentinels that stood in the desolate landscape.

While traveling north across Arizona, we visited the beautiful canyon country, the Painted Desert and the Grand Canyon.

We spent several days sightseeing around that breathtaking country before going on to the Glen Canyon Dam and Utah. We traveled on to Salt Lake City, the Great Salt Lake and then the Salt Lake Desert. They were all so beautiful in their own way. Only God could have created that tremendous landscape.

June 18th, a Sunday morning found us in Elko, Nevada. We set up camp and found what we thought would be an appropriate church. It was a cold, dry service and the doctrine was strange to us, although it was a mainline denomination. Puzzled, we went on our way.

We went on to Winnemucca, Nevada for family visits. We enjoyed being with my sister and her husband for the day. They took us up to the top of a mountain. It was a breathtaking drive on a tiny trail. It was absolutely beautiful with white aspen trees, and snow on the mountain tops.

Traveling on west, I remember how beautiful Lake Tahoe was. It appeared suddenly nestled in the basin where Nevada and California meet. Driving westward still trying to use the less traveled roads when we could, we headed for the Pacific coastline.

We reached the coast around one hundred fifty miles north of San Francisco on June 21st. It was a breathtaking trip across California on a curving mountain road. The Pacific in northern California has a beautiful rocky rugged shore, so different from our sandy northern Gulf Coast of Florida.

The water varied from light to dark blue green that day, and it was spectacular. The rocky cliffs were sometimes very high as we traveled north, trying to stay close to the shoreline.

Along the way we explored the giant redwood forests. These giant beautiful trees and forests were a special treat. On the forest floor grew spectacular large ferns, unlike any we had ever seen.

Cutting back to the coastline north of Eureka, we again marveled at the rocky shore and beautiful beige sand.

We followed the shoreline north towards Oregon before turning inland.

I often wonder how anyone could not see the perfect hand of God when we view His glorious creations. We praised Him often for what He has done and for the privilege of visiting that beauty.

In his hand are the deep places of the earth: the strength of the hills is his also. The sea is his, and he made it: and his hands formed the dry land. O come, let us worship and bow down: let us kneel before the LORD our maker. Psalms 95:4-6

We traveled on through Oregon and Washington, following a beautiful rushing creek or small river for a long portion of the highway. It turned cool for the first time. We dug out the jackets and sweaters and camped one night along that river.

In the northwest and Canada, we visited more churches along the way. Perhaps we just made poor choices, but usually we were disappointed with the services. Very few had Sunday school or night services. If they had altars, they were covered with silk or plastic flowers, having no signs of use. The services seemed very formal and programmed.

We were accustomed to a different type of church service, with necessary tissue boxes on the altars. It did teach us that worship comes in all different forms, and that people are indeed different in their own type of worship. We prayed that we would not be too critical, or be tempted to judge others based on our experiences.

We enjoyed Oregon and Washington and the beauty of these states. It was beautiful country with mountains, lakes, and spectacular wooded areas.

Chapter Six
Canada

REMEMBER

And Moses said unto the people, Remember this day, in which ye came out from Egypt, out of the house of bondage; for by strength of hand the LORD brought you out from this place:... Exodus 13:3

God wants us to see His strength in this world He has created. He provides and makes a way as long as He remains our Lord and King. Remember what He has done and how He brought us out.

Entering into that beautiful country, we quickly realized the border guards were very strict about their post. Entering into Canada was a serious thing and was only permitted on their terms.

This was before the days of terrorist bombings or shootings, yet they carefully guarded their border entrance. Because of all the shootings and terrorists attacks happening today, we would feel comforted by their carefulness. Mallory was glad he hadn't brought any extra guns besides his hunting rifles. Everything had to be declared and shown.

One of the first priorities after crossing the border was finding a place to exchange our money for what we thought would be enough Canadian money to get us across the country. We were a bit naïve. First of all, the exchange rate was poor at the time and our American money certainly wasn't equal to the Canadian funds. Mallory joked that the Canadian money looked to him like monopoly money, and because it did we didn't realize how much we were spending. Even though we didn't do a lot of souvenir shopping, just the necessities were more expensive.

We had to find at least two more banks or places to exchange money before we left Canada.

We had purchased the necessary fishing licenses so we could fish along the way, and almost every day we spent time fishing as we found lakes, ponds and streams everywhere. It was interesting to learn about the different northern fish, and we tried to educate ourselves about the necessary and different baits and lures.

Our entry point into Canada was Sumas, Washington. From there we headed north towards Dawson Creek, where the Alcan (Alaska Canadian) Highway officially begins.

British Columbia is a beautiful place, the scenery is spectacular with snowcapped mountains and mountain lakes. We often would stop just to appreciate the beauty that God had created.

There were a few commercial campsites available, but most often we camped along the numerous streams or lakes. We loved to camp at the edge of construction or gravel sites. The roads needed a lot of constant repair, so this type of place was always available. We always saw a lot of wildlife near these cleared sites. Rarely did we see any 'no camping' or 'no trespassing' signs. There was just so much beautiful country and everyone along the way just found a spot that suited them.

We did have a lot of company going north. Even though the road covered hundreds and hundreds of miles, Alaska was, and still is, a very desirable destination for summer travelers. There were a lot of RVs, campers of every description, cars, trucks and every other kind of vehicle.

Mallory loved to find a tiny little trail, which he called a dirt road, and follow it until it wound up usually at a stream of some kind where we could camp. Usually, the trail was only wide enough for a small vehicle, so we wound up with scrapes and scratches along the side of the RV and often could not turn around to get out of there so backing out was interesting the next day too.

Most of these little trails were previous fishing spots for other people and had been used to camp, often with a rock-enclosed campfire site. We loved to cook out on the campfire, but in places like this, I talked loudly and made a lot of noise to avoid the possibility of large furry visitors inviting themselves to dinner.

Traveling north through Canada, we took the necessary stops for laundry or dumping the tank of the RV, also filling up with water, because most often the place where we stopped didn't have these facilities.

The lakes along the way were so beautiful. We enjoyed many of them. We also enjoyed following the rivers. In the northern part of British Columbia we drove along Liard River and stopped at Liard River Hot Springs.

It was a beautiful area, and moose often came to drink at the springs.

The hot springs were open year-round and supposed to be extremely beneficial for arthritis. Mallory was having a lot of pain in his knees from this very affliction. The water temperature was around 110°.

We hadn't counted on his sensitive nose and the strong smell of the mineral waters. We bravely rolled up our blue jeans and waded in, but he stayed only long enough for a picture. Almost immediately after the picture, he climbed right back out saying, "It stinks!" So much for the arthritis cure, it wasn't for him.

We entered into the Yukon Territory on June 29th. There were beautiful lakes and scenery all the way. We could see glaciers on the mountains and snow on the mountaintops in the distance. We had mountain views of the St. Elias Range. The clouds often enveloped the mountains, and sometimes the roads, as we traveled through them at those high elevations.

Rocks:

Living in North Florida near the Gulf of Mexico, we don't have a lot of rocks in our area. I love rocks. On the trip to Alaska, near the streams and along the way, I would pick up pretty, colorful rocks, mostly small to medium sized and tuck them away in little nooks and crannies in the RV, not realizing just how many I had,… until later.

Rocks and stones have been used throughout the Bible to refer to items of substance and stability. This stability points to the unchanging permanence of our God, always there, whatever the need.

In *Psalms 61:2*, David calls out to God. *"From the end of the earth will I cry unto thee, when my heart is overwhelmed; lead me to the rock that is higher than I."*

He relied on the permanence of the rock that was stronger and much more stable than he. He cried out to God to let him totally rely on that solid rock-like cliff that towered above him. He recognized his own frailty in relying on that One whose strength knew no bounds.

Rocks were part of the creation of earth. Unlike humans, they are in a solid state and much more permanent than the flesh-and-blood human bodies we live in. The earth's outer solid layers are made of rock. God wanted this earth to stand until His purpose is complete.

It's very understandable that David would liken a rock to the holy God we serve. In the human mind, a towering rock cliff would serve as protection, strength and stability.

Over and over in scripture, rocks are spoken of as solid, unmoving, permanent. They could withstand flood, fire, winds and wear.

In *Psalms 62:2*, David wrote: *He only is my rock and my salvation; he is my defense. I shall not be greatly moved.*

It is said of our salvation that **we can move away from God but He won't move away from us.** He is stable, firm and always there when we call out His name. David said 'He only'. Too often in this world of self-promotion we want to depend on ourselves first instead of Him. Or we want to kind of co-depend on Him and our own self. But His way is the right way, and we very often make mistakes when we decide to do it ourselves.

Chapter Seven
Critters

REMEMBER

I will therefore put you in remembrance, though ye once knew this, how that the Lord, having saved the people out of the land of Egypt, afterward destroyed them that believed not. Jude 1:5
    Never forget that our God is a righteous judge. He loves everyone and wants all to come to Him, but he also deals with rebellion when certain ones refuse to believe him or turn away from Him.

And God said, Let the waters bring forth abundantly the moving creature that hath life and fowl that may fly above the earth... Genesis 1:20 And God said, let the earth bring forth the living creature after his kind... Genesis 1:24

Bears:
    Most of the wildlife we saw at a distance, and wished we had a good telephoto lens and better photography skills.
    We saw the first 'Beware of Bears' sign and realized we might see more than the few smaller bears from North Florida that occasionally made the news. In British Columbia, we did see our first bear. It was just a small black bear crossing the road and then ducking quickly into the brush when he noticed us. Several others were spotted during our travels.

Grizzlies or brown bears were plentiful at Denali. Larger and heavier than the black bears, they are sometimes more dangerous to humans. The females have one to four cubs every other year and they are very protective of their little ones and will attack if they feel threatened.

Grizzlies are normally solitary, active animals but they gather in large numbers along streams, lakes and rivers when the salmon are spawning. They can range in size from a female around 150 pounds to a male which can be over 700 or 800 pounds. They have a pronounced hump on their shoulders which usually distinguishes them from the black bears.

Moose:

Camped overnight at one of the numerous construction sites, we saw our first young moose exploring the hills of sand and gravel. Later moose sightings would be an every-day thing. One large one on the outskirts of Anchorage was walking around a small pond and drew a huge crowd of tourists in RV's on the side of the highway. He nonchalantly posed for many pictures, not at all bothered by the attention.

Moose were easily the animals that we saw the most. They seemed to be everywhere, and they just ignored people. I think everyone knew the moose far outweighed them and left them alone.

In downtown Kenai, we took a lot of pictures of a young moose exploring a used car lot. I guess he was tired of walking, and looking for a good deal on a car!

Mountain goat:

We spotted a mountain goat, or Stone Mountain goat, as they are also called, in British Columbia near Fort Nelson which was a rare sighting we were told. He didn't pose long. They usually choose not to be seen.

Birds and other Fowl:

We loved all the winged varieties. They have so many birds, ducks and geese, over 400 species and all so beautiful. Most are the migrating birds from the south that spend their summers there.

The state bird of Alaska is the willow ptarmigan, brown in the summer and camouflage white during the winter. We saw a lot of these, often with their babies running alongside. Feathers cover their entire legs and feet.

Beautiful little birds called puffins lived along the coastal cliffs and in the crevices of the rocks and along the shoreline. Both the tufted and horned puffins are found in the North Pacific. They are mostly black or black and white with orange-red feet and bright orange beaks during the breeding season. Their little strut-walk is so cute. They feed on small marine life and can be very vocal.

Eagles:

Alaska has an abundant supply of magnificent eagles. They were wonderful to watch. In some areas there would be an eagle perched in the top of every tall spruce tree.

An in-depth study of the eagle and its life teaches us many lessons. If they become sick with a type of food poisoning, they fly to a high rock and spread themselves out and let the sun drench them until the poisons are released. I can't help but think of how we need to go to that highest 'Rock' when we have been poisoned and burdened down by the things of this life. How we need to spread ourselves with confession before Him and let Him cleanse us and make us clean again.

Come unto me, all ye that labour and are heavy laden, and I will give you rest. Matthew 11:28

Mosquitoes and bugs:

We could almost write a book about the mosquitoes. They made their first appearance in British Columbia. We were only a short distance from the RV, looking at a little stream and a beautiful waterfall dumping into it.

We were deciding whether to try a little fishing at the spot or move on, when suddenly the monsters hit. Now we know all about mosquitoes, coming from Florida, we thought. But we didn't know anything about these super-huge things. They were vicious and almost immediately we were covered with welts.

We learned to wear long sleeves, and always keep the can of super strong repellant spray in our hands. We were too busy trying not to scratch our bites to even think about fishing anymore that day. Later, we often saw people with mosquito netting and wished we had brought Mallory's hat with the bee netting over the face. The Alaskan mosquitoes are not only known for being large, they are also noisy. You can hear them buzzing, and if they stop buzzing, look out! The buzzing stops when they've found a spot to bite you.

The Alaskans joked about how, in some spots, the mosquitoes were so bad they just carried off the people to eat as a midnight snack. They also call them their unofficial state bird.

Almost as bad as the mosquitoes were the no-see-ums, a miserable little insect that was also really annoying in certain areas. They usually came in clouds of hundreds.

Since our lives usually revolved around the outdoors, we were always covered in repellent spray.

Prairie dogs:

In the Yukon, before entering Alaska we came across a deserted small town and of course we had to explore. The log buildings were abandoned and some were falling or almost falling down.

The surprising thing we found was a large prairie dog village, and they were quite tame. They stood and begged for food and chattered at us. Obviously others had stopped to visit the town and the 'residents' learned that these tourists would share food with them. We found them to be adorable. We didn't try to touch them but they took food from our hands.

Caribou:

The caribou adults average 200-400 pounds. They are a beautiful, stately animal. The domestic kinds in Alaska are called reindeer. Both male and female grow antlers. They are a herd animal and must keep moving to find adequate food. The large herds sometimes migrate up to 400 miles between their summer and winter ranges. Some of the small herds might not migrate. We saw them most often in the open tundra.

Ice Worms:

Ice worms? Oh No! That's what we thought, too. But we received our education about them at the Begich Boggs Visitor Center at Portage Glacier in Girdwood, which is south of Anchorage. Before you pick up a chunk of that beautiful blue glacier ice and decide to taste it, be assured that there <u>are</u> ice worms, and they spend their entire lives in glacial ice. They avoid the sunlight and come to the surface in the evening or morning, and they feed on snow algae. These tiny worms are segmented and are usually less than ½" long. They function best at 0 degrees.

The visitor center has many exhibits and one of them shows the ice worm. We decided the blue ice probably wouldn't taste very good.

Dall sheep:

Dall sheep were not seen at very close range. Usually they looked like little white flecks on the mountain cliffs. They are a beautiful, majestic animal.

The white color is for their protection in the winter time when they feed at lower elevations; it's easier for them to blend into the snow. In the summer they retain their white coat, but they find their food is at higher elevations. They walk on two hoofed toes. This enables them to be sure-footed on the steep, rocky, uneven terrain.

The sheep are extremely graceful and have few enemies. Occasionally Bald Eagles have been known to snatch their young. Their senses are sharp and well-developed; usually they are loyal to their social group, where more than one can watch for danger or predators.

Otters, sea lions, seals, others:

The sea otter captivated my heart. They're absolutely adorable. I could watch them for hours, floating on their backs and using their stomach as their dinner table. The mothers float on their backs with their pups on their chests. They eat sea urchins, snails, clams or other shellfish, and bang them on their stomachs with rocks to open them while they are floating around. After eating, they often roll in the water to dislodge and clean up the debris and food from their stomachs. I really wished for the telephoto lens.

One time we saw two of them floating along with their arms linked around each other. Sea otters are probably my favorite of all the critters we saw on the trip.

We saw a lot of other animals along the way, like the huge sea lions and the adorable seals along the California coastline.

Fox, Wolves, Beavers, Elk:

One evening a cute little red fox ran round and round the RV.

We were running around the inside, window to window, trying to get a picture of it. While in Denali, our guide pointed out some elusive wolves.

A majestic elk gave us just a glimpse. Beavers and beaver dams were everywhere.

Chapter Eight
Alaska

REMEMBER

He hath remembered his mercy and his truth toward the house of Israel: all the ends of the earth have seen the salvation of our God. Make a joyful noise unto the Lord, all the earth: make a loud noise, and rejoice, and sing praise. Psalms 98: 3,4
  We need to remember, but we also need to praise Him in the remembering. What a wonderful witness to the entire world when we give Him the praise and adoration He deserves.

  Our excitement increased as we drove through Whitehorse and on towards Alaska. We were getting so close on that July 1st. The daylight hours were lengthy and neither of us wanted to stop driving in Canada that evening. I just kept on driving until we reached the state line.

  At 11:30 pm, we again entered the United States. The large sign welcomed us with 'Alaska' in gold letters and a light blue map of the state below it.

Only Alaska and Hawaii are not bordered by any other state. Alaska is part of the continental United States but it is not contiguous to the lower 48. It is the largest state in area, covering over 570,300 square miles and has the longest coastline of any state. Alaska's name was derived from the native Alyeska, 'The Great Land'.

No-one else was around when we entered the state. We had to prop up the camera and put the timer on to take pictures of both of us, which we often did. What an exciting day! It was a while after the picture taking before the excitement calmed down and we found a little rocky stream with a beautiful snow-capped mountain in the distance, and decided to make camp for the day.

Throughout the drive through Canada and Alaska we found 'The Milepost' an invaluable guide. It is published yearly with new updates on every mile along the way. It informed us of campsites, gas, parks and dump stations for the RV. In all the small towns, it told us exactly what was there. Along the highways, The Milepost pointed out all the attractions, as well as any hazards along the way.

It even pointed out the gravel turnouts where we could safely stop or camp. These were important as often the roads were very narrow with drop-offs and few, if any, shoulders. This was really a necessary guide in the days before electronic gadgets that keep us informed today. We always knew where we could find drinking water, pay-phones, rest areas, meals, propane and even litter barrels or dumpsters that were very important.

Bays, lakes, streams, rivers and all the waterways were spectacular to look at as we traveled. The great Northwest is very clean compared to the rest of our country. People rarely throw anything out the window to litter the highways. On the other hand, the people usually aren't as courteous as they are in the South. We found out quickly that the native Alaskans didn't like our slow RV driving, which we found necessary because of the frost heaves.

Frost heaves occur when the permanently frozen ground, or permafrost, melts in certain spots and leaves the road with a wavy up and down effect. The smaller vehicles can hit the 'waves' at a certain speed and don't feel it as badly, but RVs and larger vehicles can only go so fast without bouncing everywhere. It's kind of like a rough washboard dirt road and going faster to just hit the top of the bumps. Unlike a car, in an RV everything can come loose and bounce around when you hit really rugged roads. We quickly found that, there were no good speeds to suit our vehicle, but slower speeds were much better than the jarring effect of going faster.

We found a church service that Sunday morning in the town of Tok. They didn't have evening services and we went on towards Anchorage on the Glenn Highway. The scenery was breathtaking along the 328 miles.

The Glenn Highway provides wonderful views along the way from Tok to Anchorage. It was nice not to have a schedule, and we pulled over often to just soak in the view or try our hand at fishing in the rushing rivers, clear lakes, or numerous streams. Often we could see the salmon making their way upstream; it was a little frustrating before we learned how to catch them.

Views of Matanuska and Knit Glacier were awesome, along with the colorful rock formations created by long-ago glaciers. The Chugach and Talkeetna mountains were breathtaking with their deep blues and greens.

We loved the spruce, white aspen and birch trees that we didn't have at home. I believe we spent more time stopping and taking pictures than we did driving along most of the highways.

We dropped off our accumulated rolls of film to be developed at a shopping center at Eagle River. This became a convenient place to process our pictures as we passed through. It always seemed to be on our route every few days. We would pick up the last batch and leave them more.

The restaurants and local cafes were wonderful, and we tried to sample them several times a week. The food was more expensive than we were used to, but always delicious. I was shocked the first time I was served a platter full of food instead of the normal plate size. But I soon learned people burned many more calories with their active lifestyle and as a result, they ate larger amounts.

We couldn't begin to compete with the active Alaskan in the summertime. They made use of most of the daylight hours with numerous outdoor activities. I think they rested in the wintertime when there was a lot of darkness. We often rested a lot in the daytime and were out fishing in the night hours. It seemed like no matter what the time of day, there were people cycling, hiking, fishing, climbing, running or participating in other sports. They also seriously took advantage of the fish runs, using nets, or fish wheels or whatever was appropriate to catch and preserve what they needed for the winter months.

Berries were a delicious find along the way. We found wild strawberries, raspberries, salmonberries and blueberries; the cranberries would ripen later. We were told not to eat any of the white berries, as they were poisonous. We often found bear tracks in and near the berry patches. I liked to carry cans or something noisy to rattle and we also talked loudly.

We met a lovely lady while berry picking, and she showed us how to harvest the numerous fiddle leaf ferns, which were everywhere, and then gave us a lesson on cooking them. They were delicious.

It's no surprise that we were willing to try anything. Mallory, born in 1929, grew up in a poor family during the depression. He knew how to hunt and fish for anything he could find to put on the table. He taught me to appreciate whatever food we might find. I tried to be a good sport about it all.

I can't help but remember though, some of his experiments in food. Back at home one summer, he had heard that the commercial sea scallops were actually sting rays. So he convinced me we needed to try them. Sting rays were numerous in the bay, he caught a small one and we cut out balls from the wings and we prepared and cooked them. Yuck! It was really not so good. Unless the commercial fishermen processed them in a much different way, I can't believe that rumor was true.

In Anchorage we called a nephew who lived in the area. He came to visit and brought us frozen packets of bear and moose meat. I had no idea just how to cook it, but realizing it might be tough, we roasted and simmered in liquid to make it palatable. We found the bear to have a strong gamey taste, but as usual we were willing to try almost anything.

The wildflowers were spectacular. From the fields of bright red fireweed to the numerous decorative plantings in the towns, they grew prolifically.

The vegetable gardens were unbelievable. I had seen pictures of the huge vegetables, and it was all true. Perhaps it was due to the many hours of daylight combined with the rich glacial/volcanic soil. Whatever the reason, the fast growth and huge size of everything in the gardens was quite a sight.

Chapter Nine
Traveling Through the State

REMEMBER

To perform the mercy promised to our fathers, and to remember his holy covenant. Luke 1:72
Perhaps the most important thing we can remember as Christians is the fact of the Abrahamic Covenant, which was fulfilled with the birth, life, death, and resurrection of our Lord Jesus Christ. It was the promise to Abraham that his seed would bless the Earth because of his obedience and willingness to present his own Son as a sacrifice. Jesus Christ willingly gave His own life that we might believe upon Him and obtain eternal life. Always remember that.

Anchorage is located on Cook Inlet and Turnagain Arm. It is a sprawling city bound on the east and west by Chugach mountain range and Knit Arm off of Cook Inlet.

If the day is clear you can get a glimpse of Mount McKinley, 135 miles to the north. Construction in 1989 was non-stop in the summer months. New developments, buildings and repairs to the highway were constantly going on.

Nearly half of the state's population lives in Anchorage. It is certainly a municipality of contrasts with nice hotels and high rise restaurants that overlook huge parks and streams full of salmon. Moose often make appearances in the streets along with an occasional bear.

Anchorage is home to a pack of wolves, at least 1000 moose, 200 black bears and some brown bears around the edge of town.

Although Anchorage boasted many theaters and cultural things to do, we always just replenished our necessities, hit the laundromats and drove on through town toward our next destination.

Cook Inlet and Turnagain Arm have extremely high tides. When the tide goes out the mudflats are exposed.

They are composed of glacial silt and have a quicksand-like quality, if you dare to venture out on them. It appears to be firm, but the mud can be treacherous. When stepped on, it will not release you and when the tide comes in which is always unexpectedly the person trapped will drown.

The tides can reach 40 feet high in a short time, and when it is that extreme, it is known as a bore tide. The bore tides occur because of the length of the Turnagain Arm, and the height of the tides causes them come in as a wave.

In other parts of Alaska, we experienced mudflats along some of the fishing areas, and they also had a quicksand quality. I remember climbing out of my waders at one point to escape a muddy area. Fortunately we were able to pull the waders back out of the mud.

We wanted to take full advantage of the king salmon season, so we traveled on down into the Kenai Peninsula.

The Sterling Highway cut off of the Steward Highway and went through Soldotna, Kenai and on down to Homer. We spent a lot of time fishing this area from Coopers Landing to Homer.

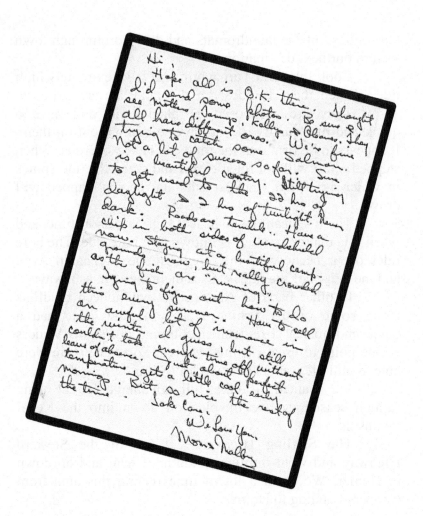

At Homer, we had our first glimpse of the damage from the 1989 Exxon Valdez oil spill which had occurred four months earlier. On March 27th , the Exxon Valdez was wrecked on Bligh Reef and spilled almost 1 million gallons of crude oil into Prince William Sound. Even though Homer was some distance from this area, there was a lot of activity going on with white-suited workers and booms collecting what little oil had made its way down towards

Homer. There were a lot of barges and ships preparing, but we didn't see much oil.

Homer is located on the north shore of Kachemak Bay, in the southeastern part of the Kenai Peninsula. We attended church there, which was held in the upstairs of a downtown store.

In Homer, we watched all the charter boats coming in with their loads of halibut and the unloading area where they hung the fish for pictures. Mallory really wanted to go out on a boat.

Mallory was determined to catch halibut, even though he knew he usually got sick in rough water. While he did fine on small boats in the bays and rivers, we knew he always got deathly ill on the rough seas, and the Gulf of Alaska is rough.

On the morning we went out, he took the prescribed nausea medicine, but unfortunately he started turning green not even 20 minutes from the shore. Then to make matters worse, he went down in the cabin to lie down.

He was advised it might get better if he stayed in the open air, but he along with quite a few others wanted to lie down and he stayed in the cabin. It was a very rough day, and there were only a few of us fishing. I kept leaving the deck to go and check on him but he just waved me away and there was nothing anyone could do until we got back to dry land. The captain wouldn't head back even though over half the fishermen were sick. I guess he was afraid some would want a refund or something.

Those of us that fished caught some nice halibut; I didn't enjoy it, knowing Mallory was miserable. When we reached the dock, he only wanted to go to the RV so we just gave them away. He recovered fine by the next day, but I'm sure the day of sickness took its toll on his weakening body.

After that, Mallory wanted to remain on the ground for a while, so we tried our hand at digging for clams. It was an area north of Homer and supposed to be good for clam digging. I don't remember if the tide was wrong or if we just didn't know how, but we didn't harvest any clams.

Soon we headed back to what would be our favorite fishing area in Alaska. From Cooper Landing along the Kenai River, down the Russian River and all around Soldotna and Kenai was a great area for us.

It was crowded with other tourists, along with the Alaskans, but we usually managed to find an out-of-the-way spot to camp and fish. In my current research I notice that a lot of areas where we camped free now charge for camping. I'm sure that brings in a lot of necessary revenue for the communities.

There were several Russian Orthodox churches. The most ornate and oldest one in Alaska was in Kenai. It was very beautiful, extremely clean and ornate, an interesting historic landmark. We toured another one in Ninilchic Village.

We meandered along the rocky coastline north of Kenai along Cook Inlet, then went back and watched the opening day of subsistence fishing. It started at midnight. It was still light and the natives were allowed to line up across the shallow river and take their fish with dip nets. At the stroke of midnight they were allowed to use their dip nets to scoop up the fish until they had their limit. Because the fish were so numerous, it really didn't take long until it was over.

Each Alaskan family has a daily and a seasonal limit of fish according to the number in the household. Our limit was different as we were sport fishing. The Alaskans needed a large amount to survive the harsh winter.

The picture above was of Mallory fighting his king salmon on the charter fishing boat.

We fished a lot from the rocky coast lines for red salmon. We lived in our fishing boots or waders, and often rain gear, because of the wet summer.

Sunday we attended church in Soldotna at one of the larger churches we found. If I remember correctly, we went back and visited this church a second time, because we spent a lot of time in the area. I think there were more tourists in the church than there were Alaskans. This was really the hot spot for the fishing season.

The charter boat out of Soldotna resulted in our two king salmon catches on the Kenai River. We didn't catch any kings from the shoreline but had a lot of fun trying. The reds were much easier to catch.

As we drove along the Seward highway we found a good stopping place where we could get a close look at a fish wheel in the river. We examined it closely to see how it worked and took pictures of it.

Heading back north, we stopped at Portage Glacier. A very interesting visitor's center is located here.

Passing through Anchorage and Eagle River again, we picked up pictures and dropped off film. We then headed north on the George Parks Highway, glimpsing occasionally the beautiful Mt. McKinley, when the clouds would allow. The highway was 358 miles from Anchorage to Fairbanks through some of the most beautiful and rugged country we had seen. The highway was paved and in pretty good condition.

Denali:

We traveled two hundred and forty miles north of Anchorage and spent a couple of days at Denali National Park. The facilities have probably changed in the last 23 years, but the park itself is protected and probably just as magnificent today as it was then. It still has just one road, which bisects the park from east to west. When we were there, only a few areas were paved on the road. It is ninety-one miles long and just one lane.

The summer temperature is comparable to most of the state with 60° - 80° in the daytime and 50°- 60° at night, with lots of rain. Before we left home, we purchased hooded good-quality rain gear for extended hours of wet outdoor use, along with boots and hip waders for mud and fishing.

The park is home to Mt. McKinley, the highest peak in North America at 20,320 feet Always snow-capped, and sometimes called the 'High One' or the 'Great One', and occasionally the 'Shy One' because of the ever-present cloud cover. Because of this, it's an absolute treat to get a glimpse of the mountain in all its glory. We took so many pictures when blessed with brief moments of sunshine. .

Denali is located in the central part of interior Alaska. The road parallels along the north side of the Alaska Range of mountains. The park has great vantage points for spectacular viewing of the center of the Alaska Range. The valley glaciers and Mt. McKinley grace many postcards and tourist brochures.

Denali now contains six million acres of wild, unfenced lands. It is the tranquil wilderness home to vast acres of tundra, glaciers and polychrome, rock-faced mountains. There are few wooded areas. The tundra consists of layers of topsoil covered by mosses, ferns, grasses and fungi. It's often spongy and waterlogged. Berry bushes thrive here and provide the numerous bears the main part of their diet.

Visitors into the park leave their own vehicles and tour the area on buses. Private vehicles are not allowed after the first few miles. Our ride was a yellow school bus. It was really very nice to be able to just look for wildlife and listen to the guide's information. The binoculars got a workout as we moved from one side of the bus to the other, searching for the animal sightings. There were extra seats on the bus, and people moved around carefully as we traveled.

We stopped often and got out when a picture-taking opportunity came up. The road often runs alongside sheer cliffs that drop hundreds of feet with no guard rails. There were also many sharp curves. I was grateful not to worry about the driving. The driver was well-trained in navigating the sharp curves and knew where the pull-outs were, in order to stop or yield to other park vehicles.

He was also a wonderfully informative guide and trained in spotting wildlife and pointing out the breathtaking scenery.

We chose the 4-hour 66-mile trip to the Eielson Visitor Center, which was 8 hours round trip. We knew that the tour would be pretty exhausting for Mallory without getting his usual rest time, but he insisted on going. Actually, the trip was so exciting, I don't think he missed his rest until we returned and he was really tired that night.

It was an exciting wonderful trip, and we decided to do it again when we returned from the Arctic area.

Denali is home to numerous animals, like grizzly bears, black bears, herds of caribou, Dall sheep, moose and gray wolves. It is also home to untold numbers of smaller animals like ground squirrels, beavers, marmots, hares and so many others. We saw many of them and loved shouting out excitedly "grizzly on the right side!" or whatever was appropriate.

Some animals are rarely seen, like the fox, lynx, martens and wolverines. The bird population is huge, with many kinds of ducks, geese, loons, and trumpeter swans, as well as the more commonly seen varieties. Many congregate at Wonder Lake but we didn't make it that far.

All of the wildlife animals and birds are protected, and feeding any wildlife is forbidden. You are encouraged to view them at a safe distance. The goal is to keep the wildlife wild.

Denali is located on part of the larger San Andreas Fault. It has at least 600 earthquakes every year. Most are too small to feel, which we were grateful for.

We saw an occasional person in the distance, and our guide informed us a few were allowed to hike and camp by permit only, but they absolutely could leave no trace in the wilderness. Everything had to be buried or carried out with them and campsites and fire pits had to be completely dismantled every day.

The next day, we enjoyed the sled-dog exhibition by the park rangers. They are such beautiful, well-trained animals. All the information about the dogs and dog-sledding was very interesting. Sled- dogs are a vital tool for survival in the wintertime for the Alaskans that live in isolated areas, as they are used for transporting, trapping and obtaining food.

~~~

North from the park entrance, we continued on toward Fairbanks. The next stop, Nenana, is located where two rivers cross, the Tanana and the Nenana. The visitor center there was located in a very picturesque sod-roof log cabin decorated with interesting artifacts and exquisite to look at with the beautiful flower beds and hanging baskets of flowers. We took quite a few pictures with the cabin as the backdrop.

Nenana is an Indian word meaning "a good place to camp between two rivers". Nenana might be best known for the annual fundraising contest with people trying to guess the exact time the ice will break up on the Tanana River. A large tripod with four supports is placed on the river ice 300' from the shore. The tripod is connected to a clock which stops when the ice goes out and moves the tripod. Other little log cabins in the area were so pretty.

Rural Native Alaskans:

Many native Alaskans are wonderful, interesting people. They hold good-paying jobs or have businesses and are the backbone of the state. In the midst of any civilization, sin will always pop up its head. God created this beautiful world. Man made it ugly and sinful.

Far too many rural Alaskans are living deep in poverty, and also living in spiritual poverty. They have sometimes been described as a desperate people. Their lives are rampant with violence, alcohol and drug abuse. Some say it was brought about by the loss of the capacity to self-govern and make decisions about how to live their lives. The roots and causes are complex and hard to understand. Some say the long, dark winter nights contribute to the suicide and alcohol abuse rate.

We were looking forward to visiting with our missionary friends in Kotzebue, to gain a better insight into this sad situation. From what we had picked up so far, we knew the missionaries had a very hard job in their mission field.

~~~

When we were traveling and stopped at an interesting spot, other people often joined us. It was interesting to visit with the other people that happened to stop there too. Often we talked to people about what God had done in our lives. It was easy and natural in that beautiful place that He created. Most of our interaction was done with other tourists or urban Alaskans.

All along the way we would stop and fish at likely streams and rivers. It was great to always have fresh fish to cook. We often cooked them over the campfire. They always seemed to taste better that way.

Sometimes, we wondered if all was well at home. Often, we just heard a little bit about a situation and not the whole story.

Chapter Ten
Fishing

REMEMBER

And remember that thou wast a servant in the land of Egypt, and that the Lord thy God brought thee out thence through a mighty hand and by a stretched out arm: ... Deuteronomy 5:15

We were slaves to sin before God saved us. What a wonderful thing God did in bringing us out and into the glorious light of the truth. Now there is eternal hope and peace in our lives because of what He did for us.

We didn't get fishing permits in the western states, but Mallory wanted to fish in Canada and, of course, Alaska so we applied for the necessary nonresident sport-fishing licenses. At first we didn't catch anything at all, but soon we learned to watch the other fishermen and talk to them about bait, lures and techniques. It seemed like each new area drove us to the local sporting goods store for different equipment.

Often we caught fish that we weren't familiar with and had to ask others what they were. Some of the fish we caught included grayling, Dolly Varden, rainbow trout and lake trout, and most of the varieties of salmon and halibut.

We began to see the salmon in the shallow streams not long after entering the state. We didn't catch any at first, but after conversations with residents and others we learned what to use for bait.

Soon we learned to make our own lures using colored yarn and the other pieces of necessary gear. Often our dining table and rest of the RV looked like a sporting goods store with all the open tackle boxes, rods and reels, and bits and pieces of all the necessary items to make the lures. The fish loved our hand-tied lures, but it got kind of messy. We just didn't have the room to organize and keep it all straight.

We did catch the salmon. We caught pinks, sockeye (reds), kings, and silvers. We fished from most of the accessible river banks, shore lines, river boats and a bay boat. The fishing was super good, exciting and available almost 24 hours with the extended daylight. We could fish whenever we chose to do so.

The great thing about the RV is we could park really close to our fishing spot where Mallory would go and rest and then fish some more. The fish processing business was really big. We sent canned salmon and a lot flash-frozen fish home to Florida by overnight shipment on dry ice.

One of the most interesting places we fished was in the middle of urban Anchorage, Ship Creek. The fishable section was only a short ½-mile long and during the king salmon season it was fascinating to see businessmen in suits and waders alongside of the always-recognizable tourists and the native Alaskans. It was combat fishing at its peak and I believe more fun to watch than to participate.

Salmon:

The instinct of the salmon to return to their place of birth at spawning time is unbelievable. Born in fresh water, they migrate to saltwater rivers, bays and the ocean, thousands of miles away. When the time comes to spawn, they must return to that specific stream or lake where they were born. Unfortunately, most of the way back is upstream, even climbing rapids and waterfalls until they reach that certain place.

They face so many obstacles and dangers. Parasites and disease can weaken them. Predators like bears, raccoons, eagles and other large birds search for an easy meal. Every type of fishing, like nets and fish wheels, and even larger fish can attack them. During the peak of their run, the fishermen line the shores of the rivers, streams and lakes. It's called combat fishing and they are literally elbow to elbow.

We were amazed at this, but usually found a gap where we tried to join them. It wasn't as enjoyable for us as it seemed to be for them. We had some fish stolen right beside us and learned to stay alert. Usually, we found an isolated place to fish and chose not to participate in the combat fishing.

The boats do the same type of combat in the water, side-by-side, with very little room to maneuver.

We already wrote about how we caught our king salmon from a chartered fishing boat. We were only allowed one per day, so we decided to take the rather expensive charter for half-a-day. That was all we needed and we did have the thrill of catching our one king each. Mallory caught his first, and decided to keep it, even though it wasn't a real large one. We were always given the choice to keep or throw it back and try for a larger one. I felt badly when my catch was larger than his. Of course it never bothered him. He was very excited for me.

The native Alaskans are allowed to use nets and fish wheels, as the fish are a necessary part of their subsistence; and it takes a lot of fish to get a family through the winter. They usually dry or can the fish to preserve them. The fish are also used to feed the sled-dogs, which are part of their lives and necessary to pull the sleds in the winter. The fish wheel is a wooden contraption in the water, fastened to the shore, that scoops up the fish as they head upstream and dumps them into a basket. We watched the fish wheels on the Copper and the Yukon Rivers. They are regulated and used by the Alaskans by special permits.

When they finally reach their spawning place, the female lays her eggs in the shallow, fine gravel. She lays up to 5,000 eggs in spawning nests called redds. The male fish fertilizes them. His job complete, he shows the signs of deterioration and the hard journey home, and soon dies. The female usually dies soon after this.

The journey of the salmon reminds me of our Christian life. You can ask any senior citizen or older person and they will tell you the journey gets much harder, the older they get.

The enemy will fight harder to reclaim a saint, knowing that their life on Earth is short. We have all the normal hazards plus many more brought on by infirmities, pain, financial problems and even the stigma of age. Often we fight an enemy that is unseen.

For we wrestle not against flesh and blood, but against principalities, against powers, against the rulers of the darkness of this world, against spiritual wickedness in high places. Ephesians 6:12

Loneliness can be a problem, too. People want to be around young, beautiful people, not those who are wrinkled, crippled and have memory problems. Loneliness can also add to the warfare when self-pity sets in.

Yes, we might have to fight harder to make it into Heaven, but we have a great bonus. We have all the years of experienced fighting and knowing how to look back and remember what He has done for us.

Chapter Eleven
More Adventures

REMEMBER

But thou shalt remember the Lord thy God: for it is He that giveth thee power to get wealth, that he may establish his covenant which he sware unto thy fathers, as it is this day. Deuteronomy 8:18
    This scripture about remembering is interesting because many believe that God will bless them with great wealth if they just ask Him to. Unfortunately, some people cannot handle wealth, and it causes them to turn away from God. He knows what we can handle much better than we do.
    The source of all wealth truly is God, and God gives us the ability to produce wealth, but people that give themselves the credit for producing wealth threaten their relationship with the Holy God. Always remember to give Him the glory for whatever ability or wealth He has blessed you with.

    We drove through Fairbanks, which is Alaska's second largest city. A brief time was spent shopping for necessary supplies and tending to laundry before moving on.

    Before we left home, one daughter gave us a roll of quarters for toll roads, and a book of stamps. We used all the stamps for postage on postcards. Quarters became a very important item to us. Every Sunday afternoon we tried to call several of our children, and often my mother or a friend, to keep track of what was happening at home. Remember, no cell phones. We didn't even have phone cards.

Laundromats were also extremely necessary. Our winter clothing was fairly heavy and often muddy with our outdoor lifestyle so laundromats were a staple in our travels.

When in the urban areas, that duffel bag full of clothes was a never-ending part of the 'city' life. Mallory usually took a nap while the clothing was being taken care of. Then he would be ready to view the landscape when we hit the road again.

With a sense of anticipation, we would head out again towards the next interesting spot. We really preferred the wild, majestic country compared to the few cities, and didn't spend a lot of time in them, but sometimes it was necessary.

Fairbanks is located 576 miles north of Anchorage. It straddles the Chena River, close to where it runs into the Tanana River. The winters are long and cold with lots of snow. The summers are short and rainy. Average winter temperatures can be -15° to -25°, and the summer can range from 50° to 70°. Fairbanks is the transportation center for interior Alaska, with roads, rail and airlines servicing the area.

The Pipeline

Hills to the north of Fairbanks get higher towards the White Mountains. We followed the Steese Highway a short ways to Fox, where we picked up the Elliot Highway and went on north toward the Arctic Circle, intending to go as far as we could toward Prudhoe Bay. It was still early in August and we planned to travel through all of the state then go home in late September or early October before the winter set in.

It was near the town of Fox that the highway started to run alongside the Trans-Alaska Pipeline. Oil is the number one industry in Alaska, followed by tourism and fishing. The pipeline, with a diameter of only 48", runs 800 miles through sometimes very rough terrain, from Prudhoe Bay to Valdez. Valdez is the northernmost ice-free port in North America. The pipeline is privately owned by the Alyeska Pipeline Service Company.

The pipeline faced many challenges during it's construction. Built between 1974 and 1977, it had to be strong enough to endure the climate and also protect the environment. There was an oil crisis in 1973 that caused a sharp spike in oil prices. The 1968 oil discovery at Prudhoe Bay helped remove the legal challenges to constructing the pipeline. There were wide-range difficulties with the construction, most of them concerning the extreme climate and the isolated terrain.

The pipeline couldn't be buried underground because of the permafrost. At some places at the North Slope, the permafrost is 1,200 to 2,000 feet deep. The heat from a buried pipeline would be around 100°. It would have melted the permafrost in areas and cause the soil to be unstable. To prevent this type of problem, the pipeline was insulated and supported above the ground. It was built in a zigzag fashion to withstand the severe temperature ranges.

The engineers also carefully considered the impact of the pipeline on the wildlife. From what we observed, the wildlife didn't appear to be disturbed at all. We saw animals all along and around the pipeline, just tending to their own business and ignoring it. This land is home to thousands of caribou. The opponents to the pipeline had concerns about the pipeline interfering with the habitat of the caribou. We noticed many caribou walking under and along the pipeline. It really didn't bother them at all.

The construction of the pipeline caused a boomtown atmosphere in the cities of Fairbanks, Valdez and Anchorage. Thousands of workers came to work on the project. They were attracted by the prospect of high-paying jobs when most of the country was in a recession. The pay was good, but they had to endure very difficult conditions, with long hours and cold temperatures as well as the rough terrain. The United States spent more than $8 billion to construct the pipeline and 12 pump stations. Thirty-two workers died from construction causes.

The workers had large amounts of money to spend in the boomtowns. This caused an increase in crime and illicit activities. Many of the law enforcement locals resigned their jobs because the pipeline offered much more lucrative pay as security guards. This left the cities without enough law enforcement, and unequipped to deal with the increase in crime.

The biggest police issue was the number of drunken brawls. Prostitutes and bars flourished; with prostitution came pimps, and the warring pimps caused many issues.

Theft of the pipelines tools and the theft of many of their vehicles, caused other problems. Some wound up in Miami and Mexico City.

The economy has greatly benefited from the pipeline. Before the pipeline, Alaska's personal income tax was the highest in the US at 14.5%. The Alaskans earned $5 billion in personal income. Now there is no personal income tax at all, and Alaskans earn $25 billion in personal income. It is the most tax-free state. Alaska is now reliant on taxes paid by oil producers and shippers.

To assure that the oil revenue wasn't all spent as it came in, the Alaskans created an Alaska Permanent Fund, a long term savings account, which pays an annual dividend to Alaskans from the interest earned.

Today, the maximum output of the pipeline is around 530,000 barrels per day. It takes 11.9 days for the oil to travel the entire length of the pipeline to Valdez. The Valdez Marine Terminal can store 9.18 million barrels in eighteen storage tanks. It has four tanker berths and two loading berths where the oil pumping takes place. More than 19,000 tankers have been filled by the marine terminal since 1977.

Maintaining the pipeline is constant and ongoing. Air patrols, as well as foot and road patrols, check for leaks, shifting or settling. The interior maintenance is completed by sending mechanical devices called pipeline pigs through the pipeline. One is known as the scraper pig, which removes the wax which collects on the interior of the pipeline. Other 'smart' pigs look for bending or buckling in the shape of the pipeline.

The most notable incident involving Alaska oil didn't involve the pipeline itself. It happened in March of 1989, three months before our trip. The Exxon Valdez was a loaded oil tanker bound for Long Beach, California. It struck Bligh Reef in Prince William Sound, spilling 260,000 to 750,000 barrels of crude oil. Eventually this spill covered 1,300 square miles of coastline.

While we were there, we saw a lot of environmental vehicles, and people working in preparation, but we didn't see a lot of oil. Most of it remained south and off-shore. Fishing didn't seem to be affected, and continued as usual.

~~~

Chapter Twelve
Far North

REMEMBER

Wherefore I will not be negligent to put you always in remembrance of these things though ye know them, and be established in the present truth. 2 Peter 1:12
 Peter felt a responsibility to remind his hearers what he and others had taught them concerning God's Word. We need to always remember what we have been taught, also. We know the basics in our minds, but by reading and studying, we refresh our minds and bring to remembrance the awesome truth of the Gospel.

 We continued north on the Elliott Highway until it connected to the Dalton Highway. We enjoyed following along, off and on, beside the pipeline. It was all so interesting. There was never a lot of traffic, but heading towards the Arctic Circle, it really thinned out even more.

 The long daylight hours became even longer the further north we traveled. When we reached our northernmost point, there was only a slight greying in the middle of the night, but it never became dark. Sometimes, we struggled to sleep because it just didn't seem like it was night, with only a few hours of darkness. We pinned up black garbage bags at the windows to darken the RV. The area north of the Arctic Circle is called the Land of the Midnight Sun. Our sleeping hours became really strange and we didn't see the actual sun shining all night long, but it did stay mostly daylight.

We noticed a lot more huge tanker trucks heading to and coming from Prudhoe Bay.

The dusty highway kept the RV really dirty. It was a never-ending chore just to keep the back window clear.

In 1989, we were limited to traveling just so far without a government permit, but we intended to go as far as allowed.

The 414 mile-long Dalton Highway ends at Prudhoe Bay. The climate is sub-arctic to polar. It averages 50° to 70° in the summer months, but it can actually go much lower than that. In the winter months -40° to -60° is possible.

Even if we had cell phones, there wouldn't have been any signal along the Dalton Highway. CB radios are the official method of communication.

The Dalton Highway has the longest stretch of highway in the U.S. with no services. North of Coldfoot, there is a 240-mile stretch without any gas stations, or services of any kind.

We began this journey completely trusting God to care for us. We both felt the peace of God surrounding us along the way. If we knew or thought about the lack of facilities, I don't remember being at all concerned about it. In researching this area, I read where the nearest hospital or medical facility of any kind was in Fairbanks.

It never entered our minds to be concerned about this. I would think about this later, remembering all the isolated spots where we had traveled with no means of communication at all. God certainly knew what He was doing, as He always does. When medical services were needed by us, they were close by.

The speed limit was about 50 mph. (certainly no problem for us). Our headlights had to remain on at all times and we were told that if we did pull over we should pull far off the road, out of the way. The road was built for oil transport trucks. Trucks always had the right of way since they cannot brake or get out of the way quickly.

Traveling north, we gradually left the boreal forests or 'Northwoods'. They had contained mainly spruces or cone-bearing evergreen trees. The Northwoods are mostly undisturbed by roads and cities, which certainly describes Alaska. The tree-covered mountains gave way to a more stark beauty near the Arctic where the winters are severe.

It was incredibly beautiful terrain. I have to wonder in the midst of all the beauty that only God could have created, how anyone could doubt Him? How it is possible that one could see the breathtaking surroundings and deny that there is a God? It often seemed that every spectacular view was placed there just for us to enjoy. We could only offer Him our praises for what He had done.

On August 7th, we crossed the Yukon River on the E.L. Patton Yukon River Bridge. Like most of the rivers, it is glacier-fed. The grey silt waters are mighty and turbulent. It is almost 2,000 miles long and goes through British Columbia, the Yukon, and then Alaska, to the Bearing Sea.

The Yukon is a major watercourse, and the longest river in Alaska and the Yukon Territory. It was the main means of transportation during the gold rush of 1896-1903.

We stopped at small lakes and streams and fished for grayling. The wildlife liked to drink along the streams, and we saw lots of tracks. No matter how clear and pretty the lake or stream we knew, to carry our own drinking water. The giardia parasite was present in most of the water in Alaska and caused severe intestinal problems.

Hiking around camping areas or lakes, we usually needed to wear our waterproof boots, as the permafrost was soggy and partially melted in August.

Driving on northward, we crossed the Arctic Circle at mile post 115.

About 55 miles north of the Arctic Circle we approached Coldfoot. Coldfoot was the site of an historic mining camp. It is situated at a beautiful site at the mouth of Slate Creek and the Middle Fork Koyukuk River. It borders the Gates of the Arctic National Park in the Brooks Range. It had RV hookups, a gas station and a restaurant.

This is a major rest stop, and would be an opportune and mandatory time to fill up the gas tank. Filling up the tank was always a painful and expensive event in Alaska. Usually it was $1 or $2 more per gallon average than in the lower 48. Of course the RV only got about 9 miles per gallon. The Coldfoot gas was the most expensive we had found.

The gas was so high that Mallory decided he didn't want to fill up at Coldfoot again. He calculated just how much farther north we could go before turning around to make it back to the gas station at the Yukon River, where the gas was a little less expensive.

It seemed kind of incongruous that we were following a pipeline which pumped over 300,000 barrels a day and yet gas was hard to find and expensive. Of course, we knew the oil had to be shipped to California to be refined before it was shipped back.

This is one of the cards written on that long stretch of road and mailed from Coldfoot office before it was sent to Fairbanks. It had both places on the postmark.

At Wiseman there were a few interesting buildings. It was a deserted gold mining town, but still has an active gold mine.

Trees were few and far between; we took a picture of the farthest north spruce tree at mile 235. In 2004, this tree was killed by a vandal. It was estimated to be 273 years old.

The Brooks Range is much as it appeared hundreds of years ago, a wild and unspoiled land. We faced many steep grades driving in these mountains. It was windy, with sudden storms, and it can snow in the summertime.

We saw grizzlies, sheep and other wildlife. In the wintertime, polar bears can roam the North Slope. We didn't see any in August.

We drove on to Atigun Pass. At 4,739 feet, it is the highest point on the highway. It was the site of a former pipeline construction camp. The road was an extremely steep climb to the pass. It is the point where the Dalton Highway crosses the Continental Divide. Water flows to the Pacific Ocean or the Bering Sea. It's also the head of the Dietrich River.

This is the point where we turned around to have enough gas to make it back to the Yukon River gas station. In 1989, we couldn't have traveled the entire distance to Prudhoe Bay without a special permit, so this was a good point to turn around.

Chapter Thirteen
South Again

REMEMBER

Thou shalt not be afraid of them: but shalt well remember what the Lord thy God did unto Pharaoh, and unto all Egypt; Deuteronomy 7:18

We can fear everything from infirmities, financial collapse, danger from a multitude of things, and even the fear of death of ourselves or a loved one. Instead of being afraid of what might possibly happen, we should trust God and rely on what He has done for others, knowing He can handle anything in our lives.

Back through Fairbanks we made the necessary stops for the laundry, water, supplies and the dump station.

Although we could have driven directly south to Valdez, we chose to skip the Richardson Highway that went south toward Valdez because we loved Denali and really wanted to return for another trip through the park.

We had less rain this trip through Denali and spotted even more wildlife. The bus drivers are very accommodating, and would stop the bus whenever we asked them to, if there was a pull-over.

It was well worth returning, and very rewarding when we spotted so many animals. A favorite stop on the route is the rest stop at Polychrome Pass where the beautiful mineral-rich rocks are a variety of colors. It reminded us so much of the colors of the Grand Canyon

Traveling around the Turnagain Arm south of Anchorage we found out that Captain Cook had named this narrow extension of Cook Inlet. It was so narrow, that when he came to a dead end he was forced to 'turn again'

Leaving Anchorage on the Seward Highway, we visited a few places we had missed before like Girdwood and Potter Marsh Game Refuge which was a great spot for bird and duck watching. At Girdwood, we took this picture of the totem pole outside of one of the shops.

It was a beautiful drive on towards Seward. The Kenai Lake is a glacial lake, in a beautiful blue-green color that runs along the highway for a while.

We drove to the end of the road that went to Exit Glacier. Some of the hiking trails sounded very interesting, but we felt the hiking would be a little strenuous. The Exit Glacier is an impressive three-mile-long river of ice.

Back on the main road we enjoyed the views of Resurrection Bay and the city of Seward before turning around back towards the Sterling Highway. This is the highway that runs between the Seward Highway and goes toward Soldotna and Kenai. We were heading right back towards our favorite fishing area. Everywhere we looked was so picturesque

Before we reached the Tern Lake Junction at the Sterling Highway, we stopped at a little town called Moose Pass. Very appropriately, a young moose crossed the road right in front of us, just before the town.

At Moose Pass, we were greeted by a sign which said, 'Moose Pass is a Peaceful Little Town, if you have an axe to grind, DO IT HERE'. This was right beside a huge old grinding wheel.

We took a picture of Mallory sharpening his knife on the grinding wheel

We camped that night near Cooper Landing, along the Kenai River. The word was out that the red or sockeye salmon were running in the Russian Lake and River, so that was where he wanted to go.

The next day along the Russian fishing area, we found shoulder-to-shoulder combat fishing and people pulling fish in all along the way. We caught our share, and needed to stop again at a fish processing plant to drop them off.

The fish were big and nearing their spawning area. The waters were teeming with bright-red fish everywhere. They were shoulder to shoulder fish in 'combat swimming' mode, I guess you could call it. The fish take on different head shapes and characteristics when they spawn. Their hormones change when they enter back into freshwater. The males in some species develop a hump near their dorsal fin. Their snout grows long; the upper jaw elongates and becomes hooked. Sometimes their teeth become larger, to fight off predators.

There are unique color changes and the female's abdominal area swells with eggs. Her snout elongates slightly. They die and deteriorate very rapidly after spawning.

Convinced that the sockeye season was just about over in that area, we again returned through Anchorage to pick up the Glenn Highway towards Valdez. As usual we took our time, sightseeing, fishing and poking along at our own pace. Picking up and dropping off our pictures, we always got the double prints and enclosed extras in the letters that we constantly posted.

Some of our oohs and aahs on the Glenn Highway were at Chugach State Park at Eagle River, views of the Matanuska Valley and Matanuska Glacier and Sheep Mountain. Although we had traveled this highway coming in from Tok, the views were entirely different heading east.

At King Mountain State Wayside, on the banks of the Matanuska River, we stayed at a very nice campsite with picnic tables, fireplaces and water for the campers.

We began to see the areas where the salmon were actually spawning. One site even had an observation deck. Of course, no fishing was allowed and we certainly did not even want to fish. We did nothing to disturb the fish, just watched. They had fought hard to arrive at their spawning area and certainly deserved some peace.

Driving down towards Valdez, we went through the town of Copper Center. During the gold rush in the late 1800s, miners braved the dangerous glaciers near Valdez and came through Copper Center on their way to the gold fields. They suffered diseases and frostbite that winter. Many died, a few made it on the gold fields, and some settled in Copper Center.

Like most of the highways, there were many turnouts along the way to view the beautiful sights. We loved the many log cabins and primitive buildings. Many of the pictures were of us standing in front of unique buildings.

Many of the older log cabins along the way and off of the main road are still used as homes. If you were hiking through the wilderness and found a cabin that was empty and open, Alaskan hospitality would always permit you to stay there. That is the Alaskan way.

Any residents of the cabins would always welcome travelers and provide a meal. If you had extra supplies to leave with them that would be appreciated as 'sourdoughs' (a term for old-timers, usually Alaskan) sometimes only went to town once or twice a year.

We often spotted meat catches next to cabins. These are small log cabins built up on stilts, 8 to 12 feet in the air. They were used for storing meat or other supplies by trappers or hunters, and were built up high to protect their supplies from wolverines, bears or other marauding animals.

As we approached Glennallen, which is near the Southern junction of the Glen and Richardson Highway, we noticed Glennallen seemed to have a large native population.

They were very busy in the summertime, smoking salmon, running dogs and working in their wonderful gardens.

Turning south on the Richardson Highway, we found a familiar friend that we had traveled alongside before, the pipeline! We would follow it to where it discharged its load in Valdez.

Turnouts on the road provided beautiful views of Worthington Glacier. A little further south we stopped at Worthington Glacier State Recreation Site.
Worthington was one of the most accessible glaciers. We were able to drive almost to the face of it and walk around

and on top of all the beautiful blue ice. We took a lot of pictures.

The next stop was near Thompson Pass. The elevation is 2,771 feet. The Thompson Pass area is now home to extreme skiing enthusiasts in the winter time. It has the highest snowfall rates in the state. One winter it measured 974 inches.

The road then descended over seven miles into Keystone Canyon. Beautiful waterfalls at Bridal Veil and Horse Tail Falls graced our view.

South of here is the road which leads to the Valdez Marine Terminal. This is the southern terminal for the Trans-Alaskan pipeline. There are several glacier views near Valdez.

Chapter Fourteen
God's Preparation

> ### REMEMBER
>
> *Then they that feared the Lord spake often to one another: and the Lord hearkened, and heard it, and a book of remembrance was written before him for them that feared the Lord, and that thought upon his name. Malachi 3:16*
>
> Malachi wrote to urge the people to be faithful and devoted to God. Only a few still honored God. He spoke here of a permanent record in Heaven of those who fear God and live honoring Him. It's reassuring and beautiful to know that God honors and records our faithfulness to Him. He will remember our commitment and fidelity when we reach Heaven and stand before Him.

As we moved into the latter part of August, we both became a little travel weary. Mallory began to have more weakness and exhaustion with little exertion. The rainy weather and the constant mud was tiring and depressing.

I had a very uneasy feeling about the upcoming moose hunt. He was looking forward to it. Our missionary friends in Kotzebue were also looking forward to our visit. It was an isolated town in the far north of the state, only accessible by a long flight in a small private bush plane. We were only going for a few days.

This trip was to include the planned moose hunting trip and camping out for the hunters. I knew the terrain would be fairly rough, and even though he was excited about it, I wondered if it would be too difficult for him. He always laughed away my concerns. I knew how much he loved to hunt, and the necessary license and permit had been obtained.

He hunted deer and squirrel at home, but after his last heart attack, I was always uneasy about him roaming in the woods alone. So I learned to hunt and usually trailed along not too far behind him, when I wasn't working. This proposed hunt would be for a 1,000 pound Alaskan moose would be entirely different. He would have 4 or 5 friends with him and it sounded easy enough at home. I even gave him an expensive heavy-duty hunting rifle as his birthday present. It was much too large for hunting the small game at home, but necessary for large game. But now the entire hunting trip just didn't seem like a very good idea.

Other hints of things we heard that were happening at home with some of the children brought an uneasy feeling. Sometimes we wondered if we should even be there at all and if maybe we should head home, but deep down we knew we had a few more things to see and do because this trip wouldn't be repeated.

Around this time, we both felt an urgency to study God's Word in more depth than before. Our daily devotion time increased and praying seemed to take on a new priority in our lives.

We really didn't have a timetable, but up until now we had always thought we would head home in late September or early October.

Now that plan seemed too drawn out, and we both agreed we would visit Valdez for just a few days to fish for the silvers in the bay. It would then be time for the short trip to Kotzebue. After the hunting trip, we would head for home.

We went ahead and made reservations for the private plane that would take us to Kotzebue and purchased tickets for the ferry trip south to Seattle. We would visit the southern Alaska area from the ferry, and after reaching Seattle, we would drive on home from there.

With these preparations in place, we again felt the peace that God was in control and we could trust Him to be with us all the way.

On the last visit through Fairbanks, we were tending to one of the many necessary RV-related chores. The sites where campers could dump their black water tank were limited, and with the many summer travelers, there was always a waiting line to take care of this.

While we were waiting our turn, I was catching up with necessary housekeeping in the back bedroom and bath, I heard Mallory laughing as he called me.

Moving to the front, I noticed we were next in line and saw him watching the man in front of us. He was an older guy, maybe 80 or so, and he was wearing a beret. He was busy with his hoses at the dumping station.

"OK, what's so funny?" I asked. The man was wearing rather tight-fitting old clothes. The pants were the polyester kind in a really loud red and brown plaid. Mallory answered, "Just watch." About that time the man bent over to pull the hose out of the hole. I gasped when I saw his pants were ripped open at the back seam line and he was wearing nothing underneath. It was a large tear and quite revealing. I shook my red face and moved away from the front window, embarrassed.

Mallory kept laughing and said, "I took a picture of him!" I responded laughing with, "Oh, no! That's going to be a good one." We always kept the camera on the dash beside the front seats so it would be handy. This was truly the funniest and most unusual picture we took. I felt bad later, and wondered if the man even had another pair of pants. The camper was an older model. I also wondered for a moment if he knew about the tear, but surely he felt the breeze on his bare skin! Most likely, he just didn't even care.

We noticed that attitude a lot in other travelers. Things they probably would not do at home, they just didn't seem to care about when they were far from home.

This incident would play a role in what was ahead. Our God truly has to have a great sense of humor, and we are created in His image.

Chapter Fifteen
Final Days

REMEMBER

I will remember the works of the Lord: surely I will remember thy wonders of old. Psalms 77:11

He saved us, He transformed us, He kept us, He healed us, and not only us personally, but remember what He has done in the lives of others in the past. John said that if all the things that Jesus did should be written down, the world itself could not contain the books. *John 21:25.*

The old town of Valdez was destroyed in the earthquake of 1964. Part of the shoreline broke off into the sea. The town was abandoned and rebuilt at its present site.

There was a small bridge at the edge of town that we crossed as we drove in. We didn't know that the little bridge often flooded and was closed during heavy rains. The road was the only access in or out, except the private planes from the airfield. Although it had been raining almost every day, we still seemed to have some sunshine along with the rain, off and on. As we drove into Valdez Friday August 25rd, it began to rain rather heavily and the rain remained with us the next few days.

We pulled between two other vehicles on the edge of the fishing area. The silvers were running, and there were a lot of campers parked around the bay. We had heard that August was a bonanza for the silvers or coho salmon. Near the campsite, many people were down by the water fishing but we enjoyed a peaceful, quiet time that evening. It was sometimes exhausting to pull on all the rain gear to get ready to go out in the downpour.

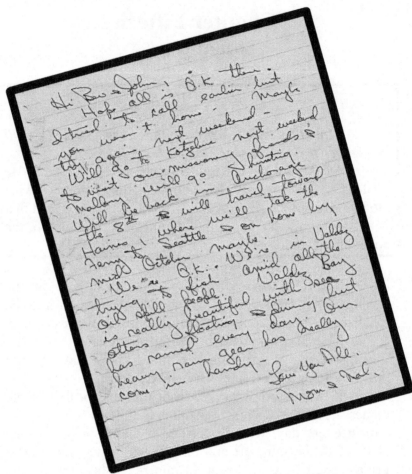

Saturday, we fished some, but the fishing wasn't that good because of all the rain. The fish were concentrated out deeper in the bay. Our limit was six fish each per day but we came nowhere near that. It was a rocky slope from the RV to get down to the water, which was also a little dangerous with the rain.

Mallory wanted to charter a boat and go out away from the shore where fishing would be better. We arranged to go out on a charter boat Monday morning, not realizing that God was orchestrating every move to bring about His will. He always does just that, but it's never been made clearer to me when I think of the events of those days.

Saturday, when we realized the fish weren't going to cooperate, we visited with other campers, went for a walk and just relaxed.

The oil spill clean-up activity was concentrated away from where we were. We saw no oil on our part of the bay. People talked about all the workers and clean-up people that were in town. We thought the portable fast-food place, brought in to help feed the crowd, was unique. It was a camper-type RV Burger King.

The otters swimming in the bay were very entertaining. We watched them from the dry interior of the RV.

It was still pouring on Sunday morning, when we set out to find a church. We found one with no difficulty, that was only a few streets away. It was a very small church and we were quite surprised to find out the church was having a revival. Even more surprising was the fact that the evangelist and his wife were from a small town in North Florida only 100 miles from our home. It's unbelievable how God arranges things.

Looking back, I can see how everything was just falling into place. We wished we had known about the revival sooner. This was the last day, and the evangelist would be flying home Tuesday, but we were happy to have found the church when we did.

The little church had a Sunday school, which was unusual compared to most of the churches. Our adult class met across the street in the pastor's tiny living room.

Inside the church, for the Sunday morning service, we saw altars at the front with tissue boxes on them. That was a real good sign that we would enjoy the service.

There was good singing. The pastor played the banjo and both he and his wife sang. The evangelist and his wife also sang. There was good music and a good message along with a very sweet, loving spirit in the church. We felt the Spirit of God moving. It was very comforting and felt like home to hear the Southern accents. We really enjoyed our Sunday.

During the afternoon we found a pay phone and made our usual check-in calls home, We never dreamed that everything would change in the next 24 hours, and the next phone calls would be entirely different.

Monday morning, more rain. We set out to find the charter boat for our last day of fishing here. After that, one day of travel to Anchorage, and then we were to catch the flight to Kotzebue.

The fishing charter was for four people, so at the dock we met the other couple that would be on our boat with us. They were very nice people, I don't remember a lot about them or where they were from. The fishing area was just a few minutes from the dock and although it was raining, the water was fairly calm on the bay. We didn't think there was a danger of Mallory getting seasick on such a small boat. It was more like fishing at home on the bays, which didn't bother him.

The gear was rigged and ready, when they handed it out and gave us instructions about the trip. The captain and his helper were very nice and stayed busy untangling lines, which happened a lot. Often we just tried to reel in our own, but it was difficult.

The rain didn't dampen our spirits. The other couple was very compatible and we joked and laughed with them. We talked about the rain and the captain said we just might not be able to leave tomorrow, as the little bridge often was closed with flooding after days of rain. It wasn't unusual at all for travelers to be stranded here. He said if we were stranded, we would need to charter another trip for the next day and catch more fish.

Mallory was in a very humorous mood and made funny faces, (as he often did), when I tried to take the picture below. Finally he let me take a good one.

The fish were biting, which kept it exciting. When the Captain said "reel in", we would turn around and pass over the area again where the fish were.

Suddenly, Mallory said "Wait!" and crumpled to the deck. He was conscious and I took the nitroglycerine from his inner pocket and gave him some. The captain called the Coast Guard ambulance and hurriedly headed back to the dock.

Mallory was not in severe pain. He held his arms over his chest but he said it was pressure, not pain. I sat on the deck of the boat and held him in my arms. I kissed him, told him I loved him and mostly just prayed for him.

He was conscious, but didn't talk much. There wasn't any turmoil or agony on his face, instead there was a total peace, almost a surreal peace, like he was seeing something unbelievable and was not in the least concerned about what was happening. That image is impressed on my mind and would help me through the following events.

Within a very few minutes, we were at the dock and the ambulance was waiting. He lost consciousness before they placed him in the ambulance, and I don't believe he ever regained consciousness. I rode with him in the ambulance for the 2 or 3 minutes to the tiny hospital.

There was a small hallway which served as a waiting room for the ER. Waiting in that hallway alone, I remember thinking 'well, at least they're not busy'. I was the only one in the hall. Sitting there, still in my rain boots and pants, I had pulled off the jacket at some point.

People came with forms and the normal questions as to what happened and what were his medications, what kind of health problems did he have and what kind of insurance. It distracted me and helped to focus on what was necessary, for a moment.

The doctor came out and said Mallory had suffered a massive myocardial infarction and he was not responding well.

My mind was racing. It wouldn't accept what the doctor said. I was thinking, 'we'll just fly him home and he'll get well again just like he did before'. Almost incapable of prayer, I knew I needed help. Hurriedly I ran to the phone on the wall and easily found the number in the small phone book hanging below it. I called the pastor of the little church and asked them to please pray.

Only a short time had passed, I stared down the hall at the emergency room door, gripping the arms of my chair. The door opened and the doctor stepped out. He slowly turned and walked my way, not briskly, the way a doctor should walk. When he reached my chair, he said he was sorry, he had done everything he could, but my husband had died.

A man came and the doctor introduced him as the chaplain. I waited numbly, knowing that my mind was retreating into shock. I thought this chaplain would pray or at least pat me on the shoulder or something! Finally, he said slowly in a very deep formal voice, "Is there anything I can do?" Immediately I said, "Yes, please go and call that preacher down the street and ask him to come." He left quickly and probably gratefully.

They must have been on the way. It was only seconds later that they were all there, the pastor, his wife and the evangelist with his wife. They all surrounded me, praying and comforting me. The pastor's wife, Susan, wrapped me in her arms, prayed, and helped me cry. They took me to their house when we finished at the hospital. Someone went and got the RV.

Romans twelve speaks of brotherly love. *So we, being many, are one body in Christ, and everyone members one of another. (Romans 12:5)* and *Be kindly affectioned one to another with brotherly love; in honour preferring one another; (Romans 12:10)*

I was a recipient of that love. Even though my family and my church family were thousands of miles away, God provided compassionate brothers and sisters in the faith to meet desperate, immediate needs.

Susan held me in her arms while I made the necessary phone calls, helping me when I couldn't even say the words. The first call was to my oldest daughter. She is a nurse and trained to be cool and calm and get all the facts. I told her Mallory had a heart attack, and she waited to hear the rest, not wanting to ask. I just couldn't say those words, but Susan helped me to get the message across. She helped me through all the other calls, wiping my tears and helping me with words to say.

Hebrews 13:5 ...I will never leave thee nor forsake thee. That is a promise you can absolutely count on. Often, He uses other people to do what is necessary, but if you are His child and you love and serve Him, He'll never leave you. He will direct your path.

It was truly miraculous how God so marvelously began to work out all the problems and difficulties, using those wonderful people, and many other people and situations, to bring order where there was just chaos.

I was 6,000 miles from home in a tiny Alaskan town with an RV and a funeral to arrange. Somehow I had to get my husband's body and my own self back to Florida.

It was first necessary to get to Anchorage, because there was no coroner's office in Valdez, and that is where we had to go to fly out.

It was still raining, and people had been advised not to drive over that bridge at the edge of town. I was in no condition to drive at all; I had difficulty even thinking.

We were advised, that it could take up to two weeks to get Mallory's body to Anchorage because of the rain and no planes were landing at the tiny airstrip. The Valdez ambulance wouldn't go across the bridge, which was about to flood, nor would an ambulance come across it coming from Anchorage.

Plane tickets to fly out of Anchorage in late August were just about non-existent. It was the busiest time, and tickets had to be purchased weeks ahead of time.

What was I to do with the RV and all our stuff, the RV that was only partially paid for?

Oh yes, there were miles of red tape to transport a body anywhere, especially out of the state, and it all had to be done quickly.

We first gathered and prayed for God's will and God's help in taking care of all these details. I wasn't much help in praying, planning or doing anything. The shock made me so numb; it was like I was watching it all from somewhere else.

Dave, the pastor, got on the phone, and God started to perform miracles. Amazingly he got me on every flight that the evangelist and his wife would be on, all the way through to north Florida flying out the very next day. The flight actually left late in the evening, giving us time to get to Anchorage.

He then called the director of the missions department in Anchorage. This man had a large yard and said I could leave the RV there as long as it was necessary. He would winterize and do whatever was needed until I could make arrangements for it.

Dave called and got refunds for the flight to Kotzebue and the ferry trip south. He also called our friends to inform them.

The transportation to Anchorage was also arranged by this dear brother. He somehow obtained permission to transport Mallory's body to the coroner's office in Anchorage in his SUV. The missionary would drive the RV with his wife and me as passengers. We were trusting God that the bridge would still be open and would not flood by morning.

As the hours flew by that afternoon, all of the red tape was somehow taken care of. They warned me that it could take days to get his body back to Florida, but he arrived in Florida not long after I did.

Late that day, I realized that I had no luggage. There was no need for it in the RV. It was just one more detail that had to be met. Susan took me to one of the few stores in the town and they had a suitable bag.

They wanted me to use one of their children's rooms that night and try and get some rest, but I knew my mind wasn't working right and I needed time to think and plan, and to pack, as we would leave early the next morning. It's hard to move around or pack things, while the RV is moving.

I convinced them that I would rest in the RV that night, or just on their couch in the family room so I wouldn't disturb them. It was a sleepless night. It was so hard to think, do anything, or to function at all.

I did manage to get some of the necessities packed, somehow even remembering to pack Mallory's dark suit that I knew would be needed for the funeral. I also managed to find all the traveler's checks that were made out in both names but made out as either/or, which saved a lot of trouble. We had tucked them away in different places in the RV.

It was hard to focus, and I had to stop often while weeping and trying to remember what should be done. It seemed that in just a few hours my world had come crashing down.

Early the next morning, I watched as Susan gathered her five children in a circle and prayed for each one before they went to school. She spoke aloud the words of *Ephesians 6:10-18,* praying that God would protect and keep them in that dark world. I once again felt her loving, caring spirit. What precious Christians He had provided to be with me: They lived the life, and didn't just talk about it.

Susan prayed with all of us before we left. The bridge held, with the rushing water almost to the top, but not overflowing. Only later would I truly appreciate all the things God accomplished in those hours.

The drive to Anchorage was about 7 hours. Midway in the drive, while sitting and vacantly staring out the window, I began to feel the weight of what was happening. The pressure and worry set in about what needed to be done, like the funeral arrangements, the difficulty getting home, years ahead without a husband, financial situations.

How could I possibly handle it all? How would I survive without my husband, who was my dearest friend and partner in everything?

That beautiful world outside the window that we had so enjoyed just a few days before now didn't hold any enjoyment at all. Other travelers and tourists fishing and traveling the state were all going about their lives, but my life had come to a crashing standstill.

The evangelist's wife rode in the seat beside her husband. They tried to include me in their conversation, but I just couldn't follow what was said and had no desire to participate.

I sat alone at the table, staring out the window. Normally, I'm not a panicky, hysterical person and can remain fairly calm in bad situations. But that Tuesday morning, I could feel hysteria, fear and panic welling up inside of me. Sobbing, on the verge of losing control, I suddenly felt God's presence in the most loving, wonderful way. I could literally feel His arms wrapped around me and I heard Him say **"Don't you trust me, my child**?" The words were so clear, so audible; I looked to see if the couple had heard them. They appeared not to have heard anything.

All the panic, hysteria and fear in my mind drained away. I said, "Oh Lord, I trust you." I knew it was God. I also knew I wasn't capable in my own self to handle what was ahead, but I could trust him. The Bible never once said for you to 'think about it', or 'you figure it out', but over and over it says 'trust God'. He already has it under control.

I've trusted Him to this day, hitherto, until this time twenty-three years later. I have no fear that He will not continue to help me, as long as I continue to draw nigh unto Him. I've learned that trusting Him is much more than speaking the words. It means giving Him everything - your family, home, business, health and every situation that you find yourself in, and then not taking these things back into your control, but letting Him use and guide you in dealing with them.

Many times, He's had to remind me of that promise to trust Him, but He's never failed me yet, and He never will as long as I depend on Him. Even today, that moment is still so vivid and so real. It continues to guide my life.

Peace I leave with you, my peace I give unto you: not as the world giveth, give I unto you. Let not your heart be troubled, neither let it be afraid. John 14:27

As we approached Anchorage, it was late in the day and gloomy with the constant rain. I felt the darkness of my situation, but the panic and hysteria were gone. Grief, deep sadness and loss pressed in, but I knew my Lord would walk me through it.

We came into Eagle River and I remembered the film we had left at the store, as well as a couple of things I needed for the trip home. We stopped and picked up the things that were necessary, and also the developed pictures.

Driving on towards the medical examiner's office and then the mission director's home to leave the RV before going to the airport, I thumbed through the pictures, trying to occupy my mind. Many of the pictures were of him, and it was so very sad, I couldn't stop my tears.

Then, there it was! The man in the plaid polyester pants, bent over with a very obvious split in his pants and no underwear. It was so startling, and also funny. How like our heavenly Father, when I was in the depths of grief, to show me that joy would one day return and that there would still be things to laugh about.

Weeping may endure for a night but joy cometh in the morning. Psalms 30:5b Solomon wrote in Proverbs, *A merry heart doeth good like a medicine.*

It was good to know God cared enough to go through all that trouble to arrange a situation with a poor man who had no underwear and didn't know how to sew, just so that I would see that picture at that time.

The trip home seemed uneventful. It was a long trip with several plane changes and layovers. I remember crowded planes and being so severely tired, but there was no way to rest.

It was sunny that September day when the plane landed near home. My girls were waiting with open arms. One daughter drove me home and spent the night with me. My church family had cleaned and aired the house. It felt comforting, even though it was not right without him.

Looking back, it was so obvious how God took control and continued helping and guiding through those next few days and weeks with all the necessary things that had to be done. He was completely in control, and I learned to let Him be in control.

Chapter Sixteen
Entrance into Peace and Glory

REMEMBER

Who remembered us in our low estate: for his mercy endureth for ever: Psalms 136:23
The psalmist who penned this had personally experienced God's remembering him and being merciful to him. As hard as it is when life is painful, we must always remember that He is the one whose mercy will never fail. All things must happen according to God's plan, and we can endure with His love and mercy.

We all have an appointed time to die and leave this world. For Mallory, it was not the time of the bad heart attack when the doctors said there was no hope and to call in the family.

God gave him twelve years to live after that time in 1977. He had time to get his affairs in order, enjoy his place on the river and hunt and fish as much as he was able.

I've often thought that if Mallory had a choice of how to leave this world and go to Heaven that it certainly wouldn't have been after weeks of suffering in a hospital. He really hated hospitals.

God gave him the desire of his heart, to see that wonderful north country and experience all the things that went with that trip. He was a good man, a strong Christian. He loved God with all his heart and served Him faithfully.

If God had asked him, "Would you like to come home to Heaven from a fishing boat in Alaska?" He would have jumped at the chance.

I remember what old Brother Greenaway used to say about leaving this world: He said he hoped that when he was out walking one day, God would say, "Greenaway, it's a lot closer to my home now than it is yours, let's go home." We were a long way from our Florida home, maybe a little closer to Heaven, when God must have said: "Mallory, it's a lot closer to my home now than it is yours, let's go home."

There are no regrets concerning this trip. I'll never believe that it was not in God's will. It was in His perfect will.

Even in the worst of the worst of times for us, His mercy will indeed be there forever. It never fails; it can never be interrupted or changed. He carries His children through those hard days, assuring them He cares and will never leave them.

The most important thing we do in this life is to prepare for eternal life. Heaven is a prepared place for those that are prepared to go there. But how do we prepare? It's really very simple. All people on this Earth have a choice to make in their lives.

Jesus answered and said unto him, Verily, verily, I say unto thee, Except a man be born again, he cannot see the kingdom of God. John 3:3

Being born again means to accept the fact that Jesus was the child of the Holy God, He lived a sinless life, died for the sins of man and rose from the dead to sit beside His Father in Heaven. When we accept and believe that He is our Savior and ask Him to forgive our sins, eternal life is granted to us.

He that believeth on the Son hath everlasting life: and he that believeth not the Son shall not see life; but the wrath of God abideth on him. John 3:36

But as many as received him, to them gave he power to become the sons of God, even to them that believe on his name: John 1:12

Becoming a Christian means we will be different. There will be peace in our hearts and joy in our lives. Worry, anger, turmoil and strife will no longer control and rule us. It is a wonderful and blessed life. Yes, even in this difficult world of problems, sorrow, sickness and pain, we will be surrounded by peace and love, simply because Jesus will live in our hearts and help us to face the hard times.

Therefore if any man be in Christ, he is a new creature: old things are passed away; behold, all things are become new. 2 Corinthians 5:17

Some people say they don't need to receive Jesus because they are basically good moral people and they only want to depend on themselves. They don't consider themselves as sinners at all. But… God's Word tells us in **Romans 3** that **_All_ have sinned and come short of the glory of God.**

Whom having not seen, ye love; in whom, though now ye see him not, yet believing, ye rejoice with joy unspeakable and full of glory:
Receiving the end of your faith, even the salvation of your souls. 1 Peter 1:8,9

Others say it's just too hard to live the Christian life. That is just so wrong. You see, Jesus left us an instruction manual, the Bible. We're supposed to read and follow the guidelines.

Reading the Bible is a fantastic, enjoyable, experience. I normally do not read most books more than once. But, the Word of God is the exception. It's always new and always fresh, no matter how many times I've read it. The best thing is the way it applies to my life for that day, that moment and that situation. It can speak to you in your situation, also.

If you're still undecided about accepting Christ, Please study for yourself, dear reader, exactly what will happen if you refuse to accept Christ.

You might want to know just what happens to a Christian when they pass from this life and what Heaven is like.

Psalms 116:15 says: ***Precious in the sight of the LORD is the death of his saints.***

Isaiah 57:1,2 tells us that it is an entrance into peace and the righteous are taken out of the evil that is to come.

Psalms 73 assures us it is an entrance into glory.

Luke 16 reminds us that Lazarus left this life, carried by the angels. I personally felt the presence of the angels when they carried my sister to heaven. In verse *43*, Jesus told the thief on the cross that he would be with him that day in paradise.

John 14 tells us about a prepared place with many mansions, one personally prepared for each of us as long as we are prepared to go.

Philippians 1 reminds us that dying for the Christian is gain and it is a blessed departure to be with Christ.

2 Timothy 4:8 Henceforth there is laid up for me a crown of righteousness, which the Lord, the righteous judge, shall give me at that day: and not to me only, but unto all them also that love his appearing

And then what about those who grieve, who are left behind when that loved one is called home? Is there comfort in God's Word for us?

Yes, there certainly is. We're told that for Christians, death is swallowed up in victory; it is a transition to fuller life, a release from the troubles of this world, and a transition to Heavenly life and glory. Paul speaks of physical death as sleep.

For we know that if our earthly house of this tabernacle were dissolved, we have a building of God, an house not made with hands, eternal in the heavens.
2 Corinthians 5:1

If in this life only we have hope in Christ, we are of all men most miserable. 1 Corinthians 15:19

Most of all, we know that although they cannot return to us, we can go and be with them, and although we grieve, we are not alone in that grief. God strengthens, keeps us and gives us that Heavenly hope for the future.

And God shall wipe away all tears from their eyes; and there shall be no more death, neither sorrow, nor crying, neither shall there be any more pain: for the former things are passed away. Revelation 21:4

We were blessed to live out a wonderful journey. It was God's final earthly gift to Mallory, giving him his heart's desire to see that beautiful, wild country that God had created.

Chapter Seventeen
An End and a Beginning

REMEMBER

When I remember thee upon my bed, and meditate on thee in the night watches: Because thou hast been my help therefore in the shadow of thy wings will I rejoice. Psalms 63:6-7

Don't ever relegate God to just a set devotion time or just on Sunday morning or just when you are desperate. If He is always with you, even in that darkest of night, you can rejoice. You are truly blessed, (surrounded by His love) in what the past has brought and what the future will bring. Praise Him in the good. Praise Him in the bad. It's easy when He is always with you and you completely trust Him and want to be in His will.

Age 48 and widowed, I'm sure it's just as hard at any age. There were a lot of adjustments to be made. In a few weeks, I went back to work and started teaching the Sunday school class again. It's a pain and kind of loss that only one that has been through it could understand. One writer said it's like losing an arm or leg or part of your own body. You are never quite the same again. That limb can be compensated for and you learn how to do without it, but you always feel like you are crippled and missing something that can't be replaced.

I had a difficult time coming home to that dark empty house. At night, Mallory always had a light on, sometimes something cooking, and often a fire in the fireplace. I now made excuses to stay at the office, or made late appointments. Usually, when I went home, I went in the front door and directly to my bedroom, which I had remodeled. I couldn't bear that empty living room or kitchen. There were nights without sleep; that's when I wallpapered all the walls in the house.

My friends and church family were wonderful. Often I was talking to someone on the phone at 3:00 a.m. The nights were always the worst. It was nothing different from what any widow or widower goes through, but it is hard.

In October 1989, my daughter and I flew back to Anchorage to settle the affair about the RV. I couldn't continue to make the payments on it without his retirement checks. I knew I would never want to use it for recreation again.

I had contacted a dealer in Anchorage, and he agreed to sell it for me on consignment. But there remained the problem of all the personal property inside.

The colors were beautiful in October. The trees were a beautiful gold or red. Many flowers were still blooming. The snow was on all the mountaintops.

We rented a car and checked into our room at the hotel, and then went to the missionary's home. They were such nice people. I told him I wanted to donate a lot of things to missions and he said, "Just pile it in the garage and I will take care of it."

Opening the door of the RV, one of the first things I saw were Mallory's boots. I scooped them up, hugged them to my chest and cried for a while. The strange thing about grieving over someone is that you never know just when that uncontrollable grief will hit, or just what will trigger

125

it. It might be what someone says that brings back the memories, or how they say it, a certain smell, or song, or a hundred other things. Usually we grieve alone, but occasionally we lose it when someone is around. I'm sure Beverly understood, but she probably thought it was strange that I would lose control over a pair of muddy boots.

When that was over, we looked around to get an idea of what kind of supplies we would need. We bought a bunch of boxes from the post office, as they only took certain sizes for mailing, along with tape and markers to ready the boxes. The guns were a different problem. They had to be sent back a different way through a dealer, which involved loads of paperwork and more expense.

With the various preparations done, we got down to work and spent several days packing boxes and carrying supplies and miscellaneous things to the garage area to be donated.

When the rocks, I had collected, began surfacing in various drawers and cubbyholes, Beverly looked at me like I was truly crazy when I said I wanted to send them home. I think I gave in and we dumped some of the larger ones but we had several boxes of rocks packed to ship home before we were done.

When God takes you through an extremely difficult life-changing time, He always opens the door to a new and different direction for your life. His plan is usually not obvious to us and He wants us to just go forward, day by day, and trust Him.

Each day of trusting, leaning on Him and seeking His direction sometimes reveals a little more of His plan. Rarely does He show you the entire path ahead. Our days in this life are full of twists, turns and often pain, as well as joy and happiness. If we were to see the entire picture, human nature would tempt us to try and control it all ourselves. Perhaps skipping the rough places and just concentrating on the happy times would suit us more.

The obvious problem is that only happy times would leave us stuck in a deep rut. It's in the hard times and rough places that we grow and mature as Christians. Sorrow, grief and loss all help to shape us and leave us with a deeper knowledge of God's Word, **if** we go through these things leaning on Him.

The first morning Beverly and I woke up in Anchorage, we were blessed with a rare sighting of Mt. McKinley out of our hotel window. It was a beautiful sight and I was so glad she got to see it, since there wouldn't be time for her to take in many of the sights of the state. I think that was the only day of sunshine. It was cool, cloudy and every day there was more snow on the mountains creeping down to our level.

When the packing was all done, we took all the boxes to the post office and shipped them home. That was the most inexpensive way to ship things. There were other people there with stacks of boxes shipping things back to the lower 48 states, also.

When the boxes arrived home, I took Mallory's pick-up to the post office to pick them up. I'll never forget the postman helping me lift them into the pick-up from the loading dock saying, "What have you got in these anyway, rocks?" I was too embarrassed to answer him. I still have most of those rocks, a reminder of that Alaska journey home.

My life without Mallory has been a new and different life. It's been 23 years since Mallory went home from Alaska to be forever with the Lord. They've been years of growth in the Lord as I've continued to study and learn.

We sent a lot of postcards on our journey. I think if Mallory could send me a postcard today, it might say something like this…

Hi Honey,
We thought Alaska was beautiful
But you ought to see this place!
It has unspeakable beauty!
There are only sunny days with no
storms, cold, or rain.
There's never any sickness or pain
I've never felt so happy, content
or wonderful. Lots of friends are here.
It's all true!! We're living forever in
constant worship and joy.
Love you, See you soon,
                                    Mallory

HEAVEN

No postage
Necessary

Jean Mallory
Panama City
Florida

Jean Mallory, author and free-lance writer, was born in a small town in New Mexico. She has traveled extensively and makes her home in north Florida.

The mother of three daughters, she is also a grandmother and great-grandmother. Widowed since 1989, Jean is active in her church and in managing her small business. She has authored three books:

Thoughts from the Battlefield
Weapons for the Battlefield
The Ebenezer Stone

Books are available as paperback at www.amazon.com or in ebook form at http://store.theebooksale.com. Books are also available by request at most bookstores.

CPSIA information can be obtained
at www.ICGtesting.com
Printed in the USA
BVOW08s1522101117
500072BV00002B/340/P